PREPARE FOR
INSURRECTION

PREPARE FOR

INSURRECTION

Gerald McIsaac

ISBN: 978-1-963068-90-0 (sc)
ISBN: 978-1-963068-91-7 (hc)
ISBN: 978-1-963068-92-4 (e)

Library of Congress Control Number: 2024927200

PREFACE

It is now mid-November, 2024, and Donald Trump is currently the "President Elect", soon to be sworn in as President, on January 20, 2025. That madman must be stopped!

The directions for stopping Trump are contained in this manuscript. That is the reason it is being rushed to the printer. It is simply a matter of demanding that the federal elections abide by the Constitutional Law, and in particular, the Twelfth Amendment, which lays out the procedure to be followed, in all federal elections. As these procedures were *not* followed in 2024, then the election was fraudulent.

Among other things, the states have *no right* to meddle in a federal election. It is up to the Electors, and *only* the Electors, to vote for the individual, of *their choice,* for the office of President. All state laws which infringe upon the duties and privileges of those Electors, must be struck down as Unconstitutional. That is the role of the Supreme Court.

The American Democratic Republic is under attack. It must be defended. As a first step, allow the Electors to vote, in early January, for the individual, of their choice, for the Presidency.

CHAPTER 1

AMERICANS: DEFEND THE CONSTITUTION! TRUMP MUST BE STOPPED!

Donald Trump has just been convicted of thirty four felony charges. The former president is now a convicted felon. He is scheduled to be sentenced on July 11. Each conviction could result in a prison sentence of one to four years. He has also been convicted of ten charges of contempt of court.

Incidentally, those ten charges of contempt of court, involved violations of orders which were issued by a judge, commonly referred to as a "gag order". Even before the trial began, the presiding judge ordered that Trump was "not allowed to comment on potential witnesses, court staff, lawyers for the prosecution, and others connected to the case". This was later expanded upon to include the members of the jury, as well as their immediate family, and immediate family of the judge.

The judge ruled that Trump was violating that gag order, with his posts on "social media" and on his campaign web site. The penalty for defying each gag order was a thousand dollar fine, which is mere "pocket change" for a billionaire.

The mainstream press is deeply concerned that the Republican National Convention, RNC, is scheduled to take place, in Milwaukee, on July 15, a mere four days after Trump is scheduled to be sentenced. It is widely accepted that Trump, a *convicted felon,* will be nominated as the Presidential candidate, on behalf of the Republican Party, *even if Trump is in prison!*

The bourgeois journalists take great delight in conducting interviews, with various experts, including those in the field of Constitutional law. Those "legal eagles" quite cheerfully assure all viewers that convicted felons, even those who are "behind bars", which is to say in jail, can still run for the office of presidency! The sitting President can be *removed* from office, upon the conviction of "high crimes and misdemeaners", but those who are convicted of such crimes, can still *serve* as president! Bourgeois democracy!

Those same experts in Constitutional law, are careful to avoid any mention of the Twelfth Amendment to the Constitution. That is the Amendment that lays out the procedure to be followed, in all *federal* elections. I mention this for the benefit of all such experts, on Constitutional law, who may not be aware of this. Why else would they not mention it? Joking!

I deliberately emphasized the word "federal", as the Constitution makes *no* mention of any "presidential election". There are a few other words and expressions that are *not* mentioned in the Twelfth Amendment. These include "District, Popular Vote, President Elect, Vice President Elect, Running Mate, Republican Party, Democratic Party and November Election". It is also my contention that the states have *no right* to meddle in a federal election! As for those who are skeptical, I have provided a copy of the Twelfth Amendment:

"The Electors shall meet in their respective states and vote by ballot for President and Vice-President, one of whom, at least, shall not be an inhabitant of the same state with themselves; they shall name in their ballots the person voted for as President, and in distinct ballots the person voted for as Vice-President, and they shall make distinct lists of all persons voted for as President, and of all persons voted for as Vice-President, and of the number of votes for each, which lists they shall sign and certify, and transmit sealed to the seat of the government of the United States, directed to the President of the Senate;–the President of the Senate shall, in the presence of the Senate and House of Representatives, open all the certificates and the votes shall then be counted;–The person having the greatest number of votes for President, shall be the President, if such number be a majority of the whole number of Electors appointed; and if no person have such majority, then from the persons having the highest numbers not exceeding three on the list of those voted for as President, the House of Representatives shall choose immediately, by ballot, the President. But in choosing the President, the votes shall be taken by states, the representation from each state having one vote; a quorum for this purpose shall consist of a member or members from two-thirds of the states, and a majority of all the states shall be necessary to a choice. [And if the House of Representatives shall not choose a President whenever the right of choice shall devolve upon them, before the fourth day of March next following, then the Vice-President shall act as President, as in case of the death or other constitutional disability of the President.–]The person having the greatest number of votes as Vice-President, shall be the Vice-President, if such number be a majority of the whole number of Electors appointed, and if no person have a majority, then from the two highest numbers on the list, the Senate shall choose the Vice-President; a quorum for the purpose shall consist of two-thirds of the whole number of Senators, and a majority of the whole number shall be necessary to a choice. But no person constitutionally ineligible to the office of President shall be eligible to that of Vice-President of the United States."

As I have previously documented, the Electoral College was established as a *concession* to the *slave owners*. It is a remnant of *slavery!* This made possible the election of a slave owner as President. His name was Thomas Jefferson. Without the Electoral College, Jefferson would never have been elected.

That being said, the fact remains that it is the law of the land, the *Constitution!* As such, it must be respected. Perhaps it is time to remind those who have taken an *oath,* to "*preserve, protect and defend the Constitution*", that it is their *duty* to do just that! They have *no right* to disregard the Twelfth Amendment!

Since the days of the Civil War, the ruling class of capitalists, currently referred to as the billionaires, have found it convenient to disregard the Twelfth Amendment. They prefer the "Two Party System", in which, once every four years, voters are allowed to choose one of the two candidates for the Presidency, of either the Republican Party or the Democratic Party. Each of those candidates gets to "choose a running mate", the candidate for Vice President.

As this has been going on for so many years, it has now achieved the status of a "time honoured tradition". That may be. Yet that in no way changes the fact that it is *Unconstitutional!* It is further a fact that *all* federal elections, since the days of the Civil War, have been *fraudulent!*

More unpleasant facts. On July 15 of this year, the Republican Party is almost certain to nominate Trump, as their candidate for President. Just as the Democratic Party is almost certain to nominate Biden as their candidate for President. Then in November, the voters will be allowed to choose between one or the other. To be followed by the Electors being forced, by state laws, to also vote for one of them. All of which is *Unconstitutional!* The states have *no right to meddle in a federal election!* Yet that is precisely what they are going to do! *Unless they are stopped!*

Remarkably enough, this is not as difficult as it may first appear. It is simply a matter of taking them "at their word", of trying to "change the system from within".

A court challenge is required, as the courts only rule on issues that are brought before the court. Possibly the simplest way of destroying the Two Party System, is by challenging any and all state laws, which require Electors to vote for a particular candidate, for the Presidency, as well as for the Vice Presidency. I have no doubt the Supreme Count will strike down such laws, given the opportunity.

As can be well imagined, this is my less than subtle way of encouraging experts in Constitutional law, to challenge these state laws. Those attorneys who are considered to be Leftist, or even progressive, may be downright anxious to take this course of action. Otherwise, there is a strong possibility that Trump will, once again, be elected as President.

Rest assured, all working people will be watching this court procedure, just as all working people are watching the trials of Donald Trump. One down, three to go! As that is the case, we can use this to raise the level of awareness of the working class.

I deeply regret placing this burden on those attorneys. No doubt, such a court challenge involves a great deal of work, as well as a considerable amount of money. At the moment, there is simply no alternative. Or at least, none of which I am aware.

As mentioned in a previous article, those of us who are on the Left, have to get organized, to coordinate our actions. That includes raising money for "worthy causes". What cause could be more worthy than abolishing the two party system? This is to say that we need a true Communist Party. But in the mean time, we do the best we can.

Trump has to be stopped.

CHAPTER 2

TRUMP A CONVICTED FELON: "A TEST FOR US AS A COUNTRY"

All of the mainstream news outlets were following the first trial of Donald Trump. No cameras were allowed inside the courtroom, but journalists were allowed to enter. These journalists were able to send "emails" to their colleagues, which documented each event, as the trial took place. This allowed other journalists, those who were outside the courtroom, to comment upon the court proceedings.

The jury deliberated a mere few hours, before delivering a verdict, concerning all thirty four felony charges. As "Juror Number One" read the decision they had arrived at, concerning each charge, that decision was emailed to the journalists outside the courtroom. Their decision was guilty on all charges.

On behalf of one mainstream news outlet, there was a team of no less than five journalists, who reported these guilty verdicts, as they were read out to the judge. Not that it takes five people to report the news. But then, their main task was not so much reporting of the news, but that of giving the news a "proper slant".

As loyal and dedicated servants of the ruling class of monopoly capitalists, the billionaires, the bourgeoisie, it was their unofficial *duty*, to "spin" the news, in a manner which best serves that class.

It was the "News Anchor" who took the lead, in giving the proper bourgeois response to this conviction of a *former President*, and *possibly future President*. As she stated:

"This is a definitive, irreducible verdict. He can appeal, I am sure he will appeal, but this is everything the prosecution asked for. From a jury that by all accounts took this thing very, very seriously. We counted the deliberation hours down here. The test for us, *as a country*, is not about what happens on appeal, and it is not about what happens in sentencing. The test for us now *as a country* is whether or not this former president *and his allies* will have succeeded in trying to undermine the rule of law, so that people reject this as a legitimate function of the rule of law in our country. They have tried to de legitimize this judge, they have tried to de legitimize this court, they have tried to de legitimize these proceedings, they have even tried to de legitimize the laws that he was tried under. These efforts are the task that we now have *as a country*. The people involved in bringing this case, have been threatened and intimidated and had everything brought to bear against them, in a way that was designed to de legitimize this process, in the eyes of the American people. It is now in the hands of the American people to decide who will accept these efforts, or whether we will stand by the rule of law...We now know, *as a country*, what it is to put a former president on trial, and to see that trial to fruition." (my italics)

I chose to reproduce this speech, in its entirety, for a reason. That reason is not to bore the reader, not to put you to sleep, but to let people know that I am not quoting out of context. The key details I have placed in italics.

On several occasions, she made reference to "us", or "we", "as a country". It is clear that she was referring to *all* Americans, of *all classes.* Yet she made no reference to *classes!* As if *classes do not exist!* Or if they exist, all classes are *united,* in a single country! Classes certainly exist, and in a single country, but that country is absolutely *not united!*

She also made reference to the "allies" of Trump. Another evasion on the subject of classes! Those "allies" are nothing other than the members of his *class,* the monopoly capitalists, the billionaires, the bourgeoisie, as well as their loyal and devoted servants.

As for those who may object, quite reasonably, that this journalist is also a loyal and devoted servant of that same class of monopoly capitalists, I can only respond that you are right. The bourgeoisie is *divided!* The revolutionary uprising of the working class, the proletariat, has given rise to a *crisis in capitalism,* so that the ruling class of billionaires have to *change their method of rule!* They just cannot agree upon that precise change!

These are facts, just as it is a fact that America has a proud history of revolution. Just as the existence of classes is denied, so too that revolutionary history is also denied.

In August of 1918, at a time which is very similar to this, Lenin wrote a letter to American workers. Bear in mind that at that time, Communists were referred to as Bolsheviks:

"The history of modern, civilized America opened with one of those great, really liberating, really revolutionary wars, of which there have been so few, compared to the vast number of wars of conquest which, like the present imperialist war, were caused by squabbles among kings, landowners or capitalists, over the division of surplus lands or ill gotten gains. That was the war the American people waged against the British robbers who oppressed America and held her in colonial slavery, in the same way as these 'civilized' bloodsuckers are still oppressing and holding in colonial slavery hundreds of millions of people in India, Egypt and all parts of the world.

"About 150 years have passed since then. Bourgeois civilization has borne all its luxurious fruits. America has taken first place among the free and civilized nations in level of development of the productive forces of collective human endeavour, in the utilization of machinery and of all the wonders of modern engineering. At the same time, America has become one of the foremost countries, in regard to depth of the abyss which lies between the handful of arrogant multi-millionaires who wallow in filth and luxury, and the millions of working people who constantly live on the verge of pauperism. The American people, who set the world an example in waging a revolutionary war against feudal slavery, now find themselves in the latest, capitalist stage of wage slavery to a handful of multi-millionaires, and find themselves playing the role of hired thugs who, for the benefit of wealthy scoundrels, throttled the Philippines in 1898, on the pretext of 'liberating' them, and are throttling the Russian Socialist Republic in 1918, on the pretext of 'protecting' it from the Germans. ...

"The American multimillionaires were perhaps, richest of all, and geographically the most secure. They have profited more than all the rest. They have converted all, even the richest, countries into their tributaries. They have grabbed hundreds of billions of dollars. And every dollar is sullied with filth: the filth of the secret treaties between Britain and her 'allies', between Germany and her vassals, treaties for the division of the spoils, treaties of mutual 'aid' for oppressing the workers and persecuting the international socialists. Every dollar is sullied with the filth of 'profitable' war contracts, which in every country make the rich richer and the poor poorer....

"In October 1917, after the Russian workers had overthrown their imperialist government, the Soviet government, the government of the revolutionary workers and peasants, openly proposed a just peace, a peace without annexations or indemnities, a peace that fully guaranteed equal rights to all nations- and it proposed such a peace to *all* the belligerent countries.

"It was the Anglo- French and the American bourgeoisie who refused to accept our proposal; it was they who even refused to talk to us about a general peace! It was *they* who betrayed the interests of all nations; it was they who prolonged the imperialist slaughter!

"It was they who, banking on the possibility of dragging Russia back into the imperialist war, refused to take part in the peace negotiations, and thereby gave a free hand to the no less predatory German capitalists, who imposed the annexationist and harsh Brest Peace upon Russia!

"It is difficult to imagine anything more disgusting than the hypocrisy, with which the Anglo- French and American bourgeoisie are now 'blaming' us *for* the Brest Peace Treaty. The very capitalists of those countries, which could have turned the Brest negotiations into general negotiations for a general peace, are now our 'accusers'. The Anglo- French imperialist vultures, who have profited from the plunder of colonies and the slaughter of nations, have prolonged the war for nearly a whole year after Brest, and yet they 'accuse' *us,* the Bolsheviks, who proposed a just peace to all countries, they accuse *us,* who tore up, published and exposed to public disgrace the secret, criminal treaties, concluded between the ex-Czar and the Anglo- French capitalists....

"A real socialist would not fail to understand, that for the sake of achieving victory over the bourgeoisie, for the sake of power passing to the workers, for the sake of *starting* the world proletariat revolution, we *cannot* and must *not* hesitate to make the heaviest sacrifices, including the sacrifice of part of our territory, the sacrifice of heavy defeats at the hands of imperialism. A real socialist would have proved by *deeds* his willingness for 'his' country to make the greatest sacrifice, to give a real push forward to the cause of the socialist revolution." (italics by Lenin)

Allow me to stress the fact that, "America opened with one of those great, really liberating, really revolutionary wars". Allow me to also stress the fact that the American people "set the world an example in waging a revolutionary war against feudal slavery", according to Lenin. Make no mistake, coming from Lenin, that is *high praise!* The American *working people* have a revolutionary history, of which they have every reason to be proud!

Now is the time to *build* upon that rich revolutionary history! Now is the time for another *revolution!* Now is *not* the time to babble such nonsense as a "test for us as a country"! Now is the time to *overthrow* the monopoly capitalist class of billionaires! Now is the time to *smash* the existing state apparatus, and *replace* that apparatus with the *Dictatorship of the Proletariat!*

Lenin had a few more words to say, further in his article, concerning the *American proletariat, not* the *country of America!*

"The American people have a revolutionary tradition, which has been adopted by the best representatives of the American proletariat, who have repeatedly expressed their complete solidarity with us Bolsheviks. That tradition is the war of liberation against the British in the eighteenth century, and the Civil War in the nineteenth century. In some respects, if we only take into consideration the 'destruction' of some branches of industry, and of the national economy, America in 1870 was *behind* 1860. But what a pendant, what an idiot would anyone be, to deny on *these* grounds the immense, world historic, progressive and revolutionary significance of the American Civil War of 1863- 65!

"The representatives of the bourgeoisie understand that for the sake of overthrowing Negro slavery, of overthrowing the rule of the slaveowners, it was worth letting the country go through years of civil war, through the abysmal ruin, destruction and terror that accompany every war. But now, when we are confronted with the vastly greater task of overthrowing capitalist *wage-* slavery, of overthrowing the rule of the bourgeoisie- now, the representatives and defenders of the bourgeoisie, and also the reformist socialists, who have been frightened by the bourgeoisie and are shunning the revolution, cannot and do not want to understand that civil war is necessary and legitimate.

"The American workers will not follow the bourgeoisie. They will be with us, for civil war against the bourgeoisie. The whole history of the world and of the American labour movement strengthens my conviction that this is so."

This is followed by his response to the accusation that Communists have been accused of resorting to methods of terror. Lenin:

"Terror was just and legitimate when the bourgeoisie resorted to it for their own benefit against feudalism. Terror became monstrous and criminal when the workers and poor peasants dared to use it against the bourgeoisie! Terror was just and legitimate when used for the purpose of substituting one exploiting minority for another exploiting minority. Terror became monstrous and criminal when it began to be used for the purpose of overthrowing *every* exploiting minority, to be used in the interests of the vast majority, in the interests of the proletariat and semi- proletariat, the working class and the poor peasants!" (italics by Lenin)

In this passage, Lenin draws a clear distinction between *individual* acts of terror, which are to be condemned, and state terror, in which a *class of people,* and in particular, the proletariat, must exercise Dictatorship over the bourgeoisie. *After* the socialist revolution, *after* the monopoly capitalists are overthrown, *after* the existing state apparatus is smashed, and replaced with a new state apparatus, in the form of the Dictatorship of the Proletariat, *then* terror *must* be used, against that same class of monopoly capitalists. Otherwise, they will return to power, as happened in the Soviet Union and in China.

Lenin went on to say:

"Now, amidst the horrors of the imperialist war, the proletariat is receiving a most vivid and striking illustration of the great truth taught by all revolutions and bequeathed to the workers by their best teachers, the founders of modern socialism. This truth is that no revolution can be successful unless *the resistance of the exploiters is crushed.* When we, the workers and toiling peasants, captured state power, it became our duty to crush the resistance of the exploiters. We are proud we have been doing this. We regret we are not doing it with sufficient firmness and determination.

"We know that fierce resistance to the socialist revolution, on the part of the bourgeoisie, is inevitable in all countries, and that this resistance will *grow* with the growth of this revolution. The proletariat will crush this resistance; during the struggle against the resisting bourgeoisie, it will finally mature for victory and for power....

"We know that help from you will probably not come soon, Comrade American workers, for the revolution is developing in different countries, in different forms, and at different tempos (and it cannot be otherwise). We know that although the European revolution has been maturing very rapidly lately, it may, after all, not flare up within the next few weeks. We are banking on the inevitability of the world revolution, but this does not mean that we are such fools as to bank on the revolution inevitably coming on a *definite* and early date. We have seen two great revolutions in our country, 1905 and 1917, and we know revolutions are not made to order, or by agreement. We know that circumstances brought *our* Russian detachment, of the socialist proletariat, to the fore, not because of our merits, but because of the exceptional backwardness of Russia, and that *before* the world revolution breaks out, a number of separate revolutions, may be defeated.

"In spite of this, we are firmly convinced that we are invincible, because the spirit of mankind will not be broken by the imperialist slaughter. Mankind will vanquish it. And the first country to *break* the convict chains, of the imperialist war, was *our* country. We sustained enormously heavy casualties in the struggle to break these chains, but we *broke* them. We are *free from* imperialist dependence, we have raised the banner of struggle for the complete overthrow of imperialism, for the whole world to see.

"We are now, as it were, in a besieged fortress, waiting for the other detachments of the world socialist revolution to come to our relief. These detachments *exist,* they are *more numerous* than ours, they are maturing, growing, gaining more strength the longer the brutalities of imperialism continue. The workers are breaking away from their social traitors...Slowly but surely the workers are adopting Communist, Bolshevik tactics and are marching towards proletariat revolution, which alone is capable of saving dying culture and dying mankind.

"In short, we are invincible, because the world proletarian revolution is invincible." (italics by Lenin)

Now it is up to us, the modern day workers and farmers, to disregard this bourgeois nonsense, that of "being tested, as a country".

The common people of Russia, proletarians and poor peasants, "blazed the trail" for the rest of us. They did this at the expense of "enormously heavy casualties", but they did it. Now it is up to us, the modern day workers and farmers, to honor their memory, by following the trail that they blazed, by following in their footsteps.

The World Proletarian Revolution is on the horizon. Monopoly capitalism is about to be crushed, and replaced with World Scientific Socialism.

CHAPTER 3

SUPREME COURT RULES "BUMP GUNS" LEGAL

Contrary to popular belief, there is no law against owning a fully automatic weapon, in America. This includes firearms which are commonly referred to as machine guns. It is perfectly legal for law abiding citizens to own such weapons.

By definition, a machine gun is a "fully automatic, rifled auto loading firearm, designed for sustained direct fire with rifle cartridges". This is quite similar to an automatic weapon, which is defined as a "self-loading firearm that continuously chambers and fires rounds, when the trigger mechanism is activated". For all practical purposes, there is little difference, although the military may disagree with that statement.

This brings us to "bump stocks", which are available for sale on the internet. These can be attached to the stocks of semi-automatic rifles, and can be used to assist in "bump firing", by the simple act of "using the recoil of a semiautomatic firearm to fire cartridges in rapid succession". They can achieve a rate of fire of between "400 and 800 rounds per minute". These can be placed on "AR" or "AK" rifles, which are commonly available.

The Supreme Court recently struck down a federal law, banning the sale of these "bump stocks". That federal law was declared to be Unconstitutional, as it violated the Constitutional right of all Americans to bear arms.

This is significant, as it means that the Supreme Court is strictly enforcing the democratic rights of all Americans, as is guaranteed in the Constitution. Emotional appeals, to the effect that such weapons, in the hands of private citizens, can be used to commit mass murder, are being disregarded. The Constitution makes no allowances for such sentiment.

As mentioned in a previous article, it is my opinion that the best way to stop Trump, from once again becoming President, is to challenge the federal election, on the grounds that it is Unconstitutional, as it violates the Twelfth Amendment. As I have reproduced that Amendment to the Constitution, in a previous article, I will not copy it here.

The implication is that, if the current federal election laws are challenged, the Supreme Court will also rule in favor of striking down all state laws, which interfere with the right of Electors to vote for the candidates, of *their* choice, for the offices of President and Vice President. This is to say that it is far more likely that they will enforce the Twelfth Amendment to the Constitution, if asked to do so.

We can expect the legal opposition, those who support the "status quo", those who are determined that "nothing should change", to make an emotional argument. They may argue that forcing the

Electors to vote for a candidates of one of the two mainstream political parties, forms the bedrock of our democratic republic. To allow those Electors to vote for the candidates of their choice, as required by the Twelfth Amendment, would threaten our democratic republic, or some such nonsense.

As for those who consider this to be something other than a serious matter, bear in mind that those who have read "Project 2025", are of a different opinion. Even though they are not considered to be "Leftist", they are deeply concerned.

As a result of reading that "Project", those same people are aware that the supporters of Trump are determined to destroy the democratic system of government, and replace it with a Dictatorship. The "Project 2025" makes that perfectly clear. It is being referred to as a "Manifesto", in that it is a two volume, 800 page tome. It outlines the procedure to be followed, in the "first 180 days", of the anticipated presidency of Trump.

They are convinced that this "Project" will "dismantle democracy as we know it", that it will eliminate the "Constitutional system of checks and balances", within the three different branches of government, the judicial, legislative and executive. All "legal obstacles and checks on the President", are to be wiped out. This would effectively give the president, in this case Trump, the power of Dictator.

The first step involves "disabling all security cameras at the DOJ", the Department of Justice. After all, thieves love darkness! All lawyers, within the DOJ, are to be fired, as they advise the members of the FBI, concerning that which is legal. Further, the "Human Rights Department" is to focus on "fighting for White Supremacy", to deny all "people of colour, women, and LGBTQ people", any rights. As well, the FBI is to focus on violent crimes, not "White Collar" crimes. This is to say that such crimes as fraud, tax evasion, bribery and election interference, among others, would effectively become legal. These are the crimes that Trump and other billionaires, specialize in committing.

The fact that this Manifesto has been written and published, is an indication of the determination of the *supporters* of Trump, to set him up as a Dictator. Such people are not to be underestimated. They have succeeded before, they can succeed again.

These supporters are members of the class of monopoly capitalists, the billionaires, the bourgeoisie. They are determined to destroy the democratic republic, and establish a Dictatorship. As capitalism is in a state of crisis, the ruling class of bourgeoisie can no longer rule in the old way, and have to change their method of rule. A Dictatorship, with that loud mouthed fool Trump, set up as the figure head President, is one possible change.

There is a very reasonable chance that the "handlers" of Trump may manage to place him back in the White House, despite his finest efforts. Even if that convicted felon is placed behind bars, he can still run for the Presidency! He could also even *win,* especially if a little "creative" vote counting was to take place. It would not be the first time such methods were used!

As can be well imagined, this is my less than subtle way of placing pressure on the attorneys, especially those who are experts on Constitutional Law. In my opinion, possibly the best way of stopping the billionaires, from overthrowing the democratic republic, is by challenging the federal elections, on the grounds that it violates the Twelfth Amendment to the Constitution.

The members of the working class, the proletariat, are closely watching, both the trials of Trump, and the "presidential race". In the process of challenging the federal election, on the grounds that it is Unconstitutional, the members of the working class will receive a valuable education. Or at least, conscious people, Communists, can use this court challenge, to raise their level of awareness.

I deeply regret placing that burden on the few people who are not only attorneys, but experts on Constitutional Law. Such a court challenge is not only difficult, but expensive. Perhaps the Councils, otherwise known as Soviets, which have recently taken shape, can assist you with this.

The fact remains that I can think of no finer way to raise the level of awareness of the working class, while at the same time, stopping the bourgeoisie from establishing a Dictatorship, with Trump in the White House. As I have previously stated, it is essential now to prepare the working class for the approaching revolution, with the subsequent Soviet- Council- Power, and the Dictatorship of the Proletariat. Such a court challenge would go a long way towards raising their level of awareness.

CHAPTER 4

MIDDLE EAST SET TO EXPLODE

The country of Israel is very small, with a population of less than ten million people. It is also a Zionist country, in that it was created in 1948, by certain members of the Jewish faith. These particular people believe that the "Holy Land", otherwise known as "Palestine", was given to them, by God. Of course, we should all respect the personal beliefs of one another.

This in no way changes the fact that, for hundreds of years, prior to this, people of various beliefs lived together, within the land referred to as Palestine. These included Muslims, Christians and Jews. They generally respected the beliefs of each other.

That situation changed, quite dramatically, with the creation of the state of Israel, a Zionist state. The Zionists then forced countless people, whose ancestors had lived in that area for hundreds of years, to "vacate the premises". Most of these people were Muslims, and they were forced to "relocate", mainly to huge "refugee camps", in which they were forced to rely mainly on handouts. That is true to this day. This is nothing other than a form of human degradation.

Of course, over the years, those people resisted. Now we have most of those "refugees", located in two areas, the West Bank and the Gaza Strip, both controlled by Israel. The people who live in those areas, have no democratic rights.

Within the Gaza Strip, the political party Hamas is in charge. Now it is clear that they have been preparing for war, with Israel, for many years. During that time, they built some impressive tunnels, and managed to "procure" some equally impressive weapons. Even more surprising, a great many men received extensive training. This enabled Hamas to conduct the October 7, 2023 attack on Israel. This gave birth to the Israeli- Hamas War, now raging for the last nine months.

Of course, Israel responded by invading the tiny Gaza Strip, with the stated intention of "wiping out Hamas". Events have not proceeded precisely the way the Israeli's intended. They have since found themselves bogged down in an urban war. The ruins of Gaza provide Hamas with ideal defensive fortifications. The Israeli's are learning the same lesson the Nazis learned in Stalingrad!

The leaders of both Israel and Hamas have been charged with war crimes. Both are being accused of waging war on civilians, by the International Criminal Court. In particular, Israel has been accused of starving civilians in Gaza, as well as bombing them, causing the deaths of countless innocent people.

The neighboring countries are becoming ever more concerned, especially as the "conflict" has spread well beyond the borders of Israel. In particular, the "militant group" Hezbollah, which is based in the country of Lebanon, to the north of Israel, has been supporting the people of Gaza, with "missile and drone strikes". These strikes have caused a series of wildfires, as well as damage to structures in Israel, and a number of casualties.

Hezbollah is thought to have an army of possibly one hundred thousand men, and has close ties to Iran. It is also reported to have two hundred thousand missiles, as well as a great many drones. For that reason, this "threat" is being taken very seriously. It has even been suggested that these missile attacks are merely a method of testing the Israeli defense's. It has further been suggested that a "deadly war is unfolding in slow motion". Without doubt, ever more advanced weaponry has been deployed by Hezbollah, striking ever deeper into Israel.

It is significant that Israel relies heavily, on that which it refers to as an "Iron Dome" defense. This is a sophisticated network of radar that detects incoming missiles, and rockets that intercept those missiles, destroying them. Yet it is clear that some missiles and drones have managed to get through, so that the defensive system is by no means infallible.

It is thought that Hezbollah is using drones, to fly at low altitude, so that radar cannot detect them. Without doubt, certain drones, as well as some rockets, are penetrating the Israeli defense's.

Incidentally, drones that carry explosives and are designed to "crash and burn", are referred to as "suicide drones", or "kamikaze drones". By contrast, drones which are designed to monitor, or which drop explosives and then return to their base, are referred to merely as drones.

Some of those more advanced weapons, both drones and missiles, come complete with "AI", which stands for "Artificial Intelligence". This is to say that these drones come complete with computers, which are "able to perform tasks that normally require human intelligence", so that they are able to evade the Israeli military systems. As well, "modified and improved missiles", courtesy of Iran, are reported to be in the possession of Hezbollah. These are being used to good effect.

Naturally, the Israelis have responded with artillery and air strikes, within Lebanon, against Hezbollah. It is their declared intention to "push Hezbollah back from the border", by "taking necessary measures to secure the border with Lebanon", according to an Israeli spokesman.

Perhaps a little explanation is in order, as so many political parties and groups are involved.

As previously mentioned, one such party is that of Hamas, which is located mainly in Gaza, and is engaged in a full scale war with Israel. The Israelis are determined to "wipe out" Hamas.

Also in Gaza, there is the Palestinian Islamic Jihad, or PIJ, fighting alongside Hamas, against the Israeli army, referred to as the Israeli Defense Force, or IDJ.

Also as previously mentioned, to the north of Israel, in Lebanon, we have Hezbollah, a very powerful force.

These political parties, or groups, are considered to be "proxies" of Iran. It is widely assumed that they are being armed and equipped by Iran.

A proxy, by definition, has the authority to represent someone else. As that is the case, it means that they are just as determined to destroy Israel, as is Iran.

To further complicate matters, we have the Houthis, based in Yemen. They appear to be part of the Islamic Resistance Movement, based in Iraq.

If this sounds confusing, it is only because it is confusing. The one characteristic they all have in common, is hatred of Israel.

The Houthis of Yemen have determined to support the people of Gaza, by attacking ships in the "Red Sea Corridor". Or at least, they are attacking ships that are bound for Israeli ports. Several cargo ships have been struck, and possibly two have been sunk. This has had the desired effect of "disrupting global trade, causing ship owners to divert their ships", which has given rise to "cascading delays and costs through supply chains", by "forcing ships away from the Suez Canal".

It is not just commercial shipping that has been attacked, in the Red Sea. The Houthis have also been attacking an American military fleet, led by the aircraft carrier Eisenhower.

A spokesman for the American navy expressed his opinion that the assignment, of protecting shipping in the Red Sea, against the Houthis, has resulted in "one of the most intense sea battles since the Second World War. Almost daily attacks". He went on to state that "They have a lot of advanced weaponry, from their friends in Iran, and they have no problem using it".

An American Commander went on to explain that the situation is "perilously dangerous. We have only to get it wrong once. The Houthis just have to get one through".

A Houthi spokesman stated that these attacks were "in retaliation for the attacks committed against the Palestinian people, in the Gaza Strip, and in response to the American and British aggression against our country".

The United Nations, the UN, is concerned that a single "miscalculation" could lead to war, which could engulf the Middle East. The UN Security Council adopted a resolution calling for an "immediate, full and complete ceasefire".

Without doubt, their fears are well grounded. As American warships are being targeted, such a war could spread well beyond the Middle East.

A conscientious American military analyst provided an assessment of the danger involved in full scale war, in the Middle East.

In the stilted jargon, which is typical of the military, he stated that the "American military has been forced to de centralize, which makes them weaker. This is referred to as 'anti access/ area denial', or 'A2/D2'. This may well be the most difficult operational challenge the US forces will face, *over the coming decades*". (my italics)

It is significant that the American military is planning for war, over a period of decades! Not that they call it war, but "operational challenge"! And this "decades long war" will happen, *unless they are stopped!*

It is very likely that the current "Israeli- Hamas War" will soon become a "Regional War", engulfing the whole Middle East, and beyond. For that reason, it is best to know what to expect.

For the benefit of those who are not engineers and physicists, a little explanation is in order.

"Mach 1" is simply the speed of sound, and "sub sonic" is less than the speed of sound, while "supersonic" is faster than the speed of sound.

A "UAV", is an "Unmanned Aerial Vehicle", or a vehicle that flies, without anyone on board.

Missiles are classified as either "Cruise Missiles", which fly at rather low altitude, and generally at "Subsonic Speeds", less than the speed of sound, and "Ballistic Missiles", which tend to travel at "Super Sonic" speed, faster than the speed of sound, and at high altitude.

Then there is the "Circular Error Probable", or "CAP", which is a measure of accuracy, in that it gives the size of the "Circle", in which the projectile is expected to land.

The military analysts are convinced that Iran has developed a number of very advanced "weapon systems", aside from the less advanced weapons, which they have provided to their "proxies", such as Hezbollah. These more advanced weapons are being built and stored underground.

There can be no doubt that Iran has adapted to economic "sanctions", imposed by America. Certain of these sanctions have been avoided by "exploiting third party countries and black markets, using front companies and false registrations".

As a result of this, the military analysts are convinced that Iran has developed "cutting edge technology". In particular, they now have "stealth UAV's", in that these Unmanned Aerial Drones are "invisible" to radar. As well, they have managed to design "two stage solid propellant missiles", which can be "launched from mobile launchers", thought to be "long range and very accurate". Then there is the "Electro Magnetic Rail Gun", perhaps the first of its kind, exceptionally powerful, with no need for an explosive propellant.

These are the weapons that Iran is keeping "in reserve". In case of "Regional War", we can expect those same weapons to be used. It remains to be seen just how well the Israeli and American defense's stand up to these weapon systems.

Unless, of course, as previously mentioned, *they are stopped!* With that in mind, consider that which Lenin wrote in 1917, at the time of the first great slaughter of working people, referred to as the First World War:

"The war is not a product of the evil will of rapacious capitalists, although it is undoubtedly being fought *only* in their interests, and they alone are being enriched by it. The war is the product of half a century of development of world capitalism and of its billions of threads and connections. It is *impossible* to slip out of the imperialist war and achieve a democratic, non-coercive peace, without overthrowing the power of capital and transferring state power to *another* class, the proletariat." (italics by Lenin)

It is completely reasonable to expect the Israeli- Hamas War to expand, as that is the stated intention of the leaders of Israel and Hezbollah, among others. They are not joking.

Just bear in mind that, as Lenin stated, this war "is not the product of the evil will of rapacious capitalists". It is the "product" of the "development of world capitalism". The capitalists are being "enriched" by this war, through the sale of weapons and ammunition to Israel. As they see it, "nothing personal, just business".

For that reason, the capitalists have to be overthrown, and state power must be placed in the hands of the proletariat. This is referred to as the Dictatorship of the Proletariat.

In this way, we can best support the people of Palestine. With the capitalists overthrown, they will no longer be supplying the Zionists with armaments. As well, the military will not be patrolling the Red Sea, so that they will not be targeted by the Houthis.

It is in this way, and only in this way, that a "democratic, non-coercive peace", can possibly be achieved.

CHAPTER 5

ONE WEEK UNTIL FIRST PRESIDENTIAL DEBATE!

The mainstream press is currently "counting down the days", until the "First Presidential Debate", between the current president, Joe Biden, and the former president- and convicted felon! - Donald Trump. This is significant, not because two staunch defenders of capitalism are about to "go head to head", but because working class people pay strict attention to the news. We can use this to our advantage.

The ruling class of monopoly capitalists, the billionaires, the bourgeoisie, have found the "Two Party System" to be a convenient method of rule. Even though it directly *violates* the Twelfth Amendment to the Constitution, so that it is *Unconstitutional!* As I have documented this in previous articles, and reproduced that particular Amendment, there is no need to copy it here.

The fact remains that American citizens are being presented with a choice, between the candidates of two parties, for the office of the Presidency. The Democrats have chosen Biden, and the Republicans have chosen Trump. Both Biden and Trump get to choose their own "running mates", the candidates for the Vice Presidency. Then comes the farce of "Presidential Debates", followed by another farce of a popular vote, in November. As if the voters have any legal right to vote for their President and Vice President! They do not! That is the duty of the Electors! And the states have no right to meddle in a federal election! As I have documented this in previous articles, there is no need to repeat it here.

Yet as the mainstream press is focused on this "Debate", it must have the attention of countless working people. This provides conscious people with the opportunity, of raising the level of awareness of the working class, the proletariat. Those who are aware of the existence of classes, and the conflict between the classes, which is to say Communists, must seize this opportunity, before it is too late!

May I suggest that Communists post articles on social media, get in touch with their friends and anyone else who is considered to be "Leftist", and disrupt that "Debate". Perhaps posters and signs demanding the election follow the procedure laid out in the Twelfth Amendment. Feel free to be vocal. Now is not the time to be shy! Be creative! Enlist the services of celebrities! Working people pay strict attention to the opinion of celebrities!

The press is reporting that Trump has a "fifty-fifty chance" of once again becoming President. True! *Unless he is stopped!*

The best way to stop Trump, is to *force* the capitalists to abide by their own laws! That will only happen when countless working people, demand that the federal election follow the procedure laid out in the Twelfth Amendment! And *that* will only happen when their *level of awareness* is raised to another level!

Time is not on our side! The illegal November election is a mere few months away. Yet Leftist Americans, especially women, have managed to organize nationwide protests, in less time than that. Now is the time for you ladies to organize another such protest. It is to be hoped that a great many men will join in this worthy cause. And what cause can be more worthy, than demanding that the capitalists abide by their own laws?

As yet, we have no true Communist Party, Dictatorship of the Proletariat. That is the reason I have resorted to such a drastic measure. It is with the utmost reluctance that I make this request. The last thing I want to do, is to increase the burden placed upon American women. Yet desperate times call for desperate measures. Trump may, yet again, become President, and that is the very definition of a desperate situation!

Bear in mind that, at the time of his election, no one was more surprised than Trump. For that reason, he was not prepared to assume the office of presidency. Yet he still managed to do considerable damage.

This time, in anticipation of once again occupying the White House, Trump is prepared. Project 2025 has been completed. The first six months of his anticipated presidency, have been carefully planned out. Nothing is being left to chance. At the end of those six months, if all goes according to plan, Trump will effectively be established as a Dictator.

At the moment, we are living under bourgeois democracy, which is better than no democracy. Our goal is proletarian democracy, with Soviet- Council- Power, and the Dictatorship of the Proletariat. To achieve that goal, we have to raise the level of awareness of the working class. By making the proletariat aware, that the ruling class of monopoly capitalists are breaking their own laws, concerning the federal election, we are serving to raise that level of awareness, while at the same time, stopping Trump from establishing a Dictatorship. Or to put it in popular terms, "killing two birds with one stone".

Ladies, you have done it before, and you can do it again. Only this time, no half measures! Keep your "eye on the ball", if you will excuse the sports metaphor. Focus on our goal, Soviet Power and the Dictatorship of the Proletariat. After all, it is only under Scientific Socialism, that you will achieve true equality.

That involves uniting all the Councils, or "Soviets", as that is the scientifically correct term, as well as all true Leftist groups, in opposition to the billionaires. As well, we urgently need a true Communist Party, Dictatorship of the Proletariat. Now that we have the internet and a cultured proletariat, these goals are well within reach. I have complete confidence in you.

Gerald McIsaac

CHAPTER 6

CONCERNING A REPORT BY BREAKTHROUGH NEWS

here are a number of "Independent" news networks, operating on the internet. This is to say that they are not part of the mainstream press, not owned by the monopoly corporations. These are referred to as "Leftist" news outlets.

One of these news outlets is known as "BreakThrough News". It recently posted an article titled "US Imperialism in Crisis? Century of Bullying Boomerangs into Resistance On All Fronts".

It is an interesting report, and appears to be presented quite sincerely, but contains a number of serious theoretical errors. As it is quite likely that those who are just now becoming politically active, are likely to read it, those mistakes should be pointed out.

The journalist is clearly concerned with that which she refers to as "genocide in Gaza", committed by the "American Vassal state of Israel". She then raised the question, "Is the fierce resistance of the people of Gaza a sign of an imperialist system in crisis? What are the characteristics and contradictions of this US led imperialist order? Here to discuss this is …an assistant professor of law …and longtime activist, and a scholar of critical race theory, with a focus on US imperialism and its impact on domestic law. Her forthcoming book, is called, 'Imperialism, An American Story".

After that glowing introduction, the hostess stated that she wanted to talk about US led imperialism. "What are the characteristics of modern day, US led imperialism? Is this a system in crisis, if so, why?"

That is a good question, but the answer was at best, confused. The distinguished "Guest" answered, by pointing out the particular method of rule, by the American imperialists, as opposed to the method of rule, of other empires. She then proceeded to point out that American imperialism tends to rule through proxy, or' 'vassal states". These "execute the American agenda, in order to get control of a particular land and its resources". She further stated that, in her opinion, "Israel is the most important vessel state, the military arm, the proxy", and that the "Gaza War was that of colonialism". This was followed by a reference to "Islands", which she thought was of great significance. Although that is doubtful, none of this has anything to do with the question!

After this confusing statement, she did manage to get to something specific. In particular, she referred to the "originator and forefather of the intellectual history of anti-imperialist thought", that of Lenin. This was promptly followed by more confusion, in that she said Lenin wrote "Imperialism, the Last Stage of Capitalism". In fact, the title of the book is Imperialism, the Highest Stage of Capitalism.

The incorrect title of the book, is rather incidental to her main point of confusion, in which she stated that, Lenin wrote, "In the second paragraph of his volume, because of Czarist censorship, his analysis of imperialism is largely theoretical, and focused on economics. Because of censorship, he cannot speak of politics the way it should be spoken about, with regards to imperialism. So what came from that, all of the great anti-imperialist thinkers since then, have focused quite a bit on economics, and militarism as well. But the question of politics, and of the politics that under gird the imperialist project, that is receiving less attention, by the great thinkers. The American imperialist project relies heavily on politics. It would not be able to dominate the world through the dollar without politics, or use foreign aid to coerce foreign nations to do what it wants, without politics, and that has a lot to do with race and racial ideology, in addition to a host of other things. And Lenin, in that second paragraph, also talks about the law, and he cannot talk about legal system. The ICC is a political institution, among others that are upholding imperialism, and this has also not been given a lot of attention, the role of the law in upholding imperialism".

This is nothing other than an absolute muddle. In fact, the "second paragraph of the volume", to which she is referring, was *not* written by Lenin. That "second paragraph" was almost certainly the second paragraph of the *introduction*, written by an editor, to the volume written by Lenin.

This particular editor collected a number of key works of Lenin, and published them in one volume, titled The Essential Works of Lenin. That same individual then wrote an introduction to the article by Lenin, titled Imperialism, the Highest Stage of Capitalism. In the second paragraph, of that introduction, he stated that, "The book was written for open, legal publication in Russia; Lenin had Tsarist censorship in mind and devised means to circumvent it".

It is very likely that the Guest confused this introduction, by an editor, with that which was written by Lenin. She then proceeded to express her opinion that, "because of Czarist censorship", Lenin did not "speak of politics the way it should be spoken about".

This is nothing other than a distortion of one of the revolutionary theories of Lenin. In particular, she maintains that Lenin did not "speak of politics" properly.

In his work State and Revolution, Lenin warned against such attacks on Marxist revolutionary theory: "This is how history is written! This is how a great revolutionary doctrine is imperceptibly falsified and adapted to prevailing philistinism!"

The opinion of this distinguished Guest, is merely one more example of a revolutionary theory being "falsified", "adapted to prevailing philistinism". She based this falsification upon the writing of an editor, whom she confused with Lenin!

It is entirely possible that the Guest was sincere, in her misunderstanding of that which she thought Lenin wrote. But an honest mistake remains a mistake. That mistake was compounded by going "on the air", and propagating it!

In conclusion, BreakThrough News deserves credit for raising the question of American imperialism, especially as it relates to the War in Gaza. Yet to bring in a Guest who has no idea of what she is talking about, can lead only to "falsification" of revolutionary theory. Such a correct revolutionary theory, of Marx and Lenin, has to be *clarified*, not falsified!

This is all the more reason for working people to read Imperialism, the Highest Stage of Capitalism, by Lenin. In that book, workers will find the answer to the question raised by the

Hostess of BreakThrough News, that of the "characteristics of imperialism", and not just American imperialism.

As Lenin pointed out, capitalism reached the stage of monopoly, at around the beginning of the twentieth century. It was the capitalists who noticed a change in the manner of "doing business", and coined the term of "imperialism".

The capitalists did not understand these changes, nor did they care. They cared only about the fact that they were making huge profits.

It was Lenin who conducted an extensive investigation, of capitalism in its new, noncompetitive stage of monopoly, referred to as imperialism. Based on that investigation, Lenin came to a few conclusions:

"The question as to whether it is possible to reform the basis of imperialism, whether to go forward to the aggravation of the antagonisms which it engenders, or backwards, towards allaying these antagonisms, is a fundamental question in the critique of imperialism. As a consequence of the fact that the political features of imperialism are reaction all along the line, and increased national oppression, resulting from the oppression of the financial oligarchy and the elimination of free competition, a democratic petty bourgeois opposition has been rising against imperialism, in almost all imperialist countries, since the beginning of the twentieth century".

It is very likely that the "Guest" represents a member of the "petty bourgeois opposition", against imperialism. Her criticism, to the effect that "Lenin did not speak of politics the way it should be spoken about", was very likely a reference to his statement that "the political features of imperialism are reaction all along the line".

She is determined to "reform the basis of imperialism", to "go backwards, towards allaying these antagonisms", which simply cannot be done! There can be no question of going "backward", to the age of competitive capitalism! The imperialists will never allow this!

Yet Lenin also gave a very complete definition of imperialism, which is monopoly capitalism:

"But very brief definitions, although convenient, for they sum up the main points, are nevertheless inadequate, because very important features of the phenomenon that has to be defined, have to be especially deduced. And so, without forgetting the conditional and relative value of all definitions, which can never include all the concatenations of a phenomenon in its complete development, we must give a definition of imperialism that will embrace the following five essential features:

1. The concentration of production and capital developed to such a stage that it creates monopolies which play a decisive role in economic life.
2. The merging of bank capital with industrial capital, and the creation, on the basis of 'finance capital', of a financial oligarchy.
3. The export of capital, which has become extremely important, as distinguished from the export of commodities.
4. The formation of international capitalist monopolies, which share the world among themselves.
5. The territorial division of the whole world among the greatest capitalist powers is completed.

"Imperialism is capitalism in that stage of development in which the domination of monopolies and finance capital has established itself; in which the export of capital has acquired pronounced importance; in which the division of the world among the international trusts has begun; in which the partition of all the territories of the globe, among the great capitalist powers had been completed".

This is not to say that we can expect "peace and tranquility", among the imperialist powers. On the contrary, as capitalism develops, among those powers, Lenin calls attention to the "vast disparity of economic and political conditions, the extreme disparity in the rate of development of the various countries, and the violent struggles of the imperialist states". This in turn necessarily leads to "the division and *re-division* *of* the world, the transition from peaceful division to *violent* division and *vice versa*". (italics by Lenin)

The point must be stressed that monopoly capitalism, imperialism, leads to war. It cannot be "patched up"! It must be destroyed! It must be replaced with Scientific Socialism, in the form of Soviet Power and the Dictatorship of the Proletariat.

The best way to support the people of Gaza, as well as all of Palestine, is to focus on overthrowing the American imperialists. The American proletariat must become class conscious, aware of the fact that they are destined to mount a revolution, smash the existing state apparatus, and crush the monopoly capitalists, the billionaires, the bourgeoisie, under the Dictatorship of the Proletariat.

It is proper to give credit to BreakThrough News, for raising the question. The answer provided, by the "democratic petty bourgeois" Guest, is incorrect. Imperialism cannot be "reformed"! Imperialism is "reaction all along the line"! It must be destroyed!

The working class will soon provide the proper answer. Now it is up to Communists, to provide the proper direction.

CHAPTER 7

FIRST PRESIDENTIAL DEBATE OF 2024: A "TRAIN

W reck"!

On June 27, 2024, a "historic event" took place, according to the mainstream press. As they stated, "for the first time ever, a sitting president had a debate with a former president". Also according to the mainstream press, this debate was nothing short of a "train wreck"! Despite the finest efforts of the "handlers" of the president, the so called "leader of the free world", President Biden himself, managed to live up to his nick name of "Sleepy Joe".

In preparation for this "Presidential Debate", the President spent a week with his "handlers", otherwise known as coaches. These people conducted numerous "mock debates", in which Biden practiced the answers to questions, which were likely to be asked, at the Debate. Bear in mind that he was first provided with the "proper" answers.

It should be pointed out that, even though a question could be asked concerning a particular subject, such as inflation, there is no law that states the answer must have something to do with the question! All too often, the answer is merely an evasion! So a question concerning inflation, for example, can be answered with a reference to "climate change". One has nothing to do with the other! Yet that in no way changes the fact that it is an answer!

That is where the "handlers", come into play. They advise the "candidate" with not only the "proper" answers, but also the tone of voice, facial expression, posture, "body language", including the position of hands- this is considered to be of vital importance! This is referred to as "grooming" the candidate.

In most cases, this tends to work quite well, especially as the "candidate" has merely to read from a "teleprompter", one which is carefully concealed from the cameras. This teleprompter can be thought of as a television screen, and even tells the candidate when to pause, perhaps pretend to take a drink of water, for example. In this way, "all bases are covered", and the audience is properly impressed.

But then, the "audience" sees nothing of this teleprompter. Also bear in mind that the audience is nothing other than the members of the public! The same people who vote this candidate into office! Based largely upon the "impression", provided by the handlers of the candidate!

The problem was, that this "Presidential Debate" did not allow for teleprompters. What is more, the questions to be asked, were supposed to be kept secret. Whether that is the case or not, is doubtful, but that is incidental to the fact that Biden was deprived of his teleprompter. The result was disastrous! He came across as the feeble minded old man that he is! He was completely confused, consistently "lost his train of thought", mumbled and even paused, trying to remember the proper response. A "train wreck"!

As a result of this, the Democratic Party is now in "damage control", as they phrase it. The "Party line", is now that Biden merely had a "bad day", and this can "happen to anyone". As proof that he has "recovered", he is now making the "proper" speeches, reading from a teleprompter. He is determined to keep running for a second term!

There are numerous other members, of the Democratic Party, who are equally determined that Biden will *not* run for a second term. They are convinced that he will merely go "down in flames", and take the Party with him!

The Democratic Party is just as divided, as the Republican Party! Both Parties need our help! It is our patriotic duty to offer our assistance! It is the least we can do!

For that reason, as I have previously suggested, all "Leftist" people should join those two Parties, as "card carrying" members. The only requirement for such membership, is to be an American citizen, possibly eighteen years of age. Bear in mind that it is the card carrying members, of those Parties, who determine the candidates for all political offices, of those same Parties. This includes the offices of President, and Vice President.

Just consider the possibilities. If enough Leftist people join those two Parties, then both Republican and Democratic Parties can endorse the same candidates, for the offices of **both** President and Vice President. May I suggest Senator Bernie Sanders for the office of President, and perhaps Michal Moore for the office of Vice President? As the same candidates of both Parties, they can run against themselves. That should help to keep campaign finances to a minimum. Who cares which Party wins the White House? The candidates are the same.

As for those who object that I am being ridiculous, allow me to respond that the capitalists are fond of saying that, "if we do not like the way things are", then we should "change the system from within". Feel free to "take them at their word". Join the two Parties, and make every effort to enact meaningful changes. It is the least we can do.

No doubt, in turn, they will "express their appreciation", in terms which will leave "no room for any misunderstanding"! They will make it perfectly clear that the billionaires are in charge, and fully intend to remain in charge! In this way, the level of awareness, of the proletariat, will be raised.

May I further suggest that, in the interest of performing their patriotic duties, all Leftist Americans insist that the forth coming federal election, follow the procedure laid out in the Twelfth Amendment to the Constitution. No doubt, those who are responsible for these elections, are not aware of the fact that the federal election must follow that procedure. *Ha!*

Once they become aware of that fact, they will no doubt be only too happy to conduct the next federal election, according to the Constitution. *Fat chance!*

Of course, that last statement was meant as a bit of a joke, one which the capitalists do not find the slightest bit funny. Which in no way changes the fact that it is true! As I have documented this in a previous article, there is no need to repeat it here.

It will almost certainly require a Supreme Court decision, to force the capitalists to conduct a federal election, according to the Constitution. It is up to experts on Constitutional law, to challenge the next federal election, on the grounds that the current "Presidential election" is Unconstitutional.

Allow me to stress the fact that, as a result of that Presidential Debate, the situation has changed, and quite dramatically. It is now far more likely that Donald Trump, a convicted felon, will once again become President of the United States, *unless he is stopped!*

For that reason, it is ever more urgent for Leftist people, to become politically active. It is becoming increasingly apparent, that capitalism has reached a state of crisis. The capitalists can no longer rule in the old way, and now have to change their method of rule. One possible change is to that of a Dictatorship, with Trump as the figurehead President.

Lenin gave some excellent advice, concerning our current state of affairs, in his landmark work, Left Wing Communism, An Infantile Disorder. He wrote:

"The fundamental law of revolution, which has been confirmed by all revolutions, and especially by all three Russian revolutions in the twentieth century, is as follows: for a revolution to take place, it is not enough for the exploited and oppressed masses to realize the impossibility of living in the old way, and demand changes; for a revolution to take place, it is essential that the exploiters should not be able to live and rule in the old way. It is only when the *'lower classes' do not want* to live in the old way, and the 'upper classes' *cannot carry on in the old way*, that the revolution can triumph. This truth can be expressed in other words: revolution is impossible without a nationwide crisis (affecting both the exploited and the exploiters). It follows that, for a revolution to take place, it is essential, first, that a majority of the workers (or at least a majority of the class conscious, thinking, and politically active workers), should fully realize that revolution is necessary, and that they should be prepared to die for it; second, that the ruling classes should be going through a governmental crisis, which draws even the most backward masses into politics (symptomatic of any genuine revolution is a rapid, tenfold and even hundredfold increase in the size of the working and oppressed masses- hitherto apathetic- who are capable of waging the political struggle), weakens the government, and makes it possible for the revolutionaries to rapidly overthrow it." (italics by Lenin)

It is my opinion that the current situation is revolutionary. It is further my opinion that the "triumph" of the working class, in the approaching revolution, is *not yet assured!* The reason I say this, is because it is *not* clear that "the majority of class conscious, thinking and politically active workers", are aware of the fact that "revolution is necessary", and also, it is certainly *less clear* that they are "prepared to die for it".

This is my less than subtle way of suggesting that class conscious people, intellectuals, whether working class or middle class, it makes no difference, are being *negligent,* in their *duty* to raise the level of awareness of the working class, the proletariat.

Feel free to focus on that which Lenin referred to as the "Key link", as stated in his great work, What Is To Be Done? "Every question 'runs in a vicious circle', because political life as a whole, is an endless chain consisting of an infinite number of links. The whole art of politics lies in finding and taking as firm a grip as we can, of the link that is least likely to be struck from our hands, the one that is most important at the given moment, the one that most of all guarantees its possessor the possession of the whole chain."

In my opinion, the "key link" now, is to *raise* the level of awareness of the proletariat, to *prepare* them for the approaching revolution, and Scientific Socialism, in the form of the subsequent Dictatorship of the Proletariat.

Time is not on our side. It is now ever more likely that Trump will, once again, become President, within a matter of months. Only this time, he is prepared. Bear in mind that Project 2025 has been completed.

In addition to the suggestions made in this article, may I suggest that the members of all Councils get together, join forces, and create a proper Communist Party, Dictatorship of the Proletariat. As well, get in touch with "internationalist workers", those who have come together, in the absence of such a Communist Party.

The alternative, that of a "different method of rule", by the monopoly capitalists, possibly in the form of a Dictatorship, led by Trump, is not to be considered.

Gerald McIsaac

CHAPTER 8

BIDEN AND THE TWENTY FIFTH AMENDMENT TO THE CONSTITUTION

The "First Presidential Debate of 2024", held on June 27, revealed that which the "handlers" of President Joe Biden have been trying to hide. The *President is suffering from dementia!*

That is the opinion of numerous medical professionals, including those who care for people who are suffering from dementia. It is also their opinion that Joe Biden is in the somewhat later stages of dementia. The President of the United States has been mentally ill *for a considerable time!*

For the sake of those who are not medical professionals, we can say that, according to the internet, "Dementia is a term for several diseases that effect memory, thinking, and the ability to perform daily activities".

In the case of Joe Biden, these "daily activities" involve the duties that come with being the "Head of State"! He is the *President!* The very nature of the job demands the ability to think clearly! Which is the one thing that Biden *cannot* do!

It is also a fact that the"*illness gets worse over time"!* Biden is not about to recover! His ability to "remember, think and preform daily activities", are steadily declining! He is already at the point where he *gets lost in the White House!*

The political situation has changed, and changed quite dramatically, literally overnight. On June 27, the mainstream press was reporting that the age of President Biden was a "key issue", in his "bid to run for re-election". There was "some question", that an "individual of his age", could "serve another four years", as President.

That is no longer an "issue"! There can be no question of a mentally ill man, running for the office of President! Now it is a question of how to *remove* that mentally ill man, from the office of President!

I consider this to be of exceptional importance, if only because countless working people are paying strict attention. This provides us with an opportunity to raise the level of awareness of the proletariat.

Numerous people are now calling upon Biden to resign from the office of presidency. It is clear that he can no longer carry out his duties. It is also clear that he no longer has the mental capacity to understand this! His "handlers" are making those decisions for him! It is to their advantage to keep their "asset" in office! They regard Biden as their "golden goose"!

As that is the case, various people are considering the option of invoking the Twenty Fifth Amendment to the Constitution, as a means of removing the mentally ill President, from office. In particular, they are referring to Section 4:

"Section 4—Whenever the Vice President and a majority of either the principal officers of the executive departments or of such other body as Congress may by law provide, <u>transmit</u> to the President pro tempore of the Senate and the Speaker of the House of Representatives their written declaration that the President is unable to discharge the powers and duties of his office, the Vice President shall immediately assume the powers and duties of the office as Acting President."

For the benefit of those who do not keep track of Washington politics, the Vice President is Kamala Harris. The "principle officers of the executive department", is a reference to the members of the Presidential Cabinet. The "President pro tempore" of the Senate is a reference to the "longest served senior Senator of the majority party", in this case Senator Patty Murray, and the Speaker of the House of Representatives is Mike Johnson.

Clearly, it is up to the Vice President, in this case Kamala Harris, and the "Members of the Cabinet", to take action. As the President is mentally ill, unable to perform his duties, it is their *duty!*

It is significant that the Vice President and majority of Members of the Cabinet do *not* have to *prove* that the President is "unable to discharge the powers and duties of his office". They merely have to "transmit" their "written declaration" to the "President pro tempore" of the Senate, and to the "Speaker of the House"! *Nothing else!* At that point, the Vice President *"immediately"* becomes the *"Acting President"!*

Yet there is a problem, a little "hitch", if you will. The fact of the matter is that the last federal election, which placed Biden in the office of President, as well as Harris in the office of Vice President, was fraudulent! It did not follow the procedure laid out in the Twelfth Amendment! Unconstitutional! For that reason, Biden is a fraudulent President, and Harris is a fraudulent Vice President. As well, the members of his Cabinet, are equally fraudulent!

Now we have a situation in which the fraudulent Vice President, Kamala Harris, as well as the fraudulent members of the Cabinet, are being asked to remove from office, a mentally ill, fraudulent President! The word ironic comes to mind!

Yet the Twenty Fifth Amendment allows for such an event. It refers to a "majority" of "such other body as Congress may by law provide". That places the "ball in the court" of Congress! Let the Congress select a "body"! Not about to happen! The Congress specializes in doing nothing!

In the interest of raising the level of awareness of the working class, we can point out the hypocrisy of the mainstream press, as well as the vast majority of democratically elected politicians. They are well aware that President Biden is mentally ill, unable to perform his duties. They are equally well aware that he should be removed from office. Yet they choose to do nothing! Regardless of the Twenty Fifth Amendment!

They are also well aware, and are *obligated* to ensure, that all federal elections follow the procedure laid out in the Twelfth Amendment. After all, they have taken an *oath,* to *"Preserve, protect and defend the Constitution"*! They have *no right* to *disregard* the parts of the Constitution which they find to be objectionable! And the Twelfth Amendment they do not like! So they merely pretend that it does not exist!

Previously, I have suggested that legal experts, those who specialize in Constitutional law, challenge the federal election, on the grounds that it violates the Twelfth Amendment. As I have documented this in a previous article, there is no need to repeat it here.

Remarkably enough, even though all Democrats are agreed that the "Debate" was a "disaster", many of them are determined that Biden should remain in office. Not only that, they are determined that he should remain the Democratic Party candidate for President, so that he can serve for another four years!

If they have their way, voters will be forced to choose between someone who is mentally ill, and a convicted felon, a habitual liar! Guess who is likely to win!

The Presidential Debate of June 27, just made the Dictatorship of Trump, far more likely! If Trump is elected, we can "kiss our democratic rights goodbye"!

This is to stress the fact that capitalism is in a state of crisis. In such a situation, as Marx stated, " The ruling class can no longer rule in the old way, and has to change their method of rule". Their current method of rule, is the democratic republic. This provides us with certain democratic rights, those which are "truncated, restricted and distorted", according to Lenin. Yet that is better than no democratic rights at all!

This brings us to conscious people, those who are aware of the existence of classes, of the antagonism between the classes, and of the need for revolution. Of course, I am referring to Leftist people, especially Communists.

May I suggest that this is similar to the situation which existed in Russia, in the fall of 1917. At that time, the leader of the Russian

Provisional Government, Kerensky, was determined to surrender the capital city of Petrograd, to the Germans, as a means of crushing the revolution. As Lenin stated, "The impending surrender of **Petrograd** will make our chances a hundred times less favorable…History will not forgive us, if we do not assume power now"!

As for those who may suggest that I am perhaps overstating the matter, I can only respond that Project 2025 has already been prepared. Trump is all set to assume power, and set himself up as Dictator. At that point, we will lose all democratic rights, and our tasks will indeed be a "hundred times" more difficult.

Just as Kerensky had to be stopped, so too, Trump must be stopped. If he is not stopped, "history will not forgive us"! It is for that reason, I recommend court challenges, among other things. The Electors must be allowed to vote for the candidates of *their* choice, for the offices of President and Vice President. It is doubtful that many of them will vote for Trump.

As well, those previously mentioned "other things", include having the various Councils come together, to work in harmony, along with the "groups of internationalist workers", to whom Lenin refers. It is also necessary to create a true Communist Party, Dictatorship of the Proletariat.

Incidentally, at the latest trial of Trump, the press was quick to point out the appearance of a "celebrity", a "movie star". Such is the power of **celebrities**! Especially movie stars! They have merely to make an appearance! The press is bound to approach them, and ask them for their opinion! Take note, Leftist movie stars! You have the power! Use it!

It is also a fact that, it is the women who are leading the revolutionary motion, at least in America. But then, it is the women who have the most to lose, if Trump gets elected. They also have the most to gain, under Scientific Socialism, the Dictatorship of the Proletariat. They have also proven themselves to be excellent organizers.

Ladies, now is the time to build upon your previous success. In fact, it is time to prepare for an insurrection. The country is a "powder keg", and any "spark" could cause an explosion. The election of Trump, as President- God forbid! - could be that spark!

As I have gone into the preparation for an insurrection, in other articles, I will not repeat it here. I can only add that it is my most sincere hope, that fellow male chauvinists will "grow a set", and support you gallant ladies.

I deeply regret placing this burden upon you. The men should be leading this revolution. They are not. It is what it is. Yet I have complete confidence in you ladies.

As I write this, I have just learned that the Supreme Court issued a ruling, in favour of Trump. In particular, they said that "the president has immunity for official acts, but not unofficial acts". Now it is "up to the lower courts to determine the difference".

This just means more delay, in one of the trials of Trump, precisely the very thing he wants. Take note: the election of Trump, once again as president, just became more likely.

With Fraternal Communist Greetings,

Gerald McIsaac

CHAPTER 9

AMERICAN CAPITALISTS CHANGING THEIR METHOD OF RULE

The United States Supreme Court just "handed down a landmark decision", according to the mainstream press. This has been described as an "unprecedented legal shield" for Donald Trump. For once, the mainstream press "got it right"!

The Supreme Court has effectively "paved the road to the White House", for Trump! At the behest of their "lords and masters", the bourgeoisie, no doubt!

As for those who object that the Supreme Court is "impartial", may I point out that we live in a class society. For that reason, no government agency is completely impartial. All such agencies, including the Supreme Court, serve the ruling class of monopoly **capitalists**, the multi billionaires, the bourgeoisie.

Their ruling is an indication that the same bourgeoisie has come to a decision. Their days of wavering are over. Faced with a crisis in capitalism, as well as with the revolutionary movement of the working class, they are aware that their "time honored" method of rule, that of the "Two Party System", is no longer effective. They have decided to change their method of rule. This new method is to be that of a Dictatorship, led by Trump. The Supreme Court ruling leaves no room for any misunderstanding, on that point!

Certain attorneys, who are considered to be authorities on Constitutional law, are of the opinion that this gives a sitting President, as Trump once was, "absolute immunity" for "core Constitutional acts", while for other official acts, there is "presumptive immunity". There is "no immunity" for "unofficial acts". The expression "clear as mud", comes to mind!

The Supreme Court also left it to the "lower courts" to define the difference between "core Constitutional acts", "other official acts", and "unofficial acts". In popular terms, they "passed the buck"!

Trump is currently facing numerous criminal charges, for crimes he allegedly committed, while serving as President. This Supreme Court ruling provides the lawyers, who work for Trump, the opportunity to challenge all such charges, on the grounds that they were "official acts", so that Trump is "immune from prosecution".

The comparison has been made to the statement of another former President, that of **Richard** Nixon. As he put it, "If the President of the United States breaks the law, it is not a crime".

The Supreme Court has just confirmed that Nixon had it right! The President of the United States cannot commit a crime!

This Supreme Court decision also has a "ripple effect", in that it effects the actions of the "lower courts". The state of New York recently convicted Trump of thirty-four felony charges, and the date of July 11 was set, to pronounce sentence. That "date of sentencing" was immediately postponed until September, "at the earliest", and probably later. It is very likely that the presiding judge will "set aside" those felony convictions, in order to "spare the country" the "shame and disgrace" of having a presumptive "presidential candidate", who is a convicted felon.

As well, the three other trials he is scheduled to face, have also been postponed, presumably until after the "November election".

To put this in popular terms, that is "one side of the coin", but "every coin has two sides". In scientific terms, we say that it is "one side of the contradiction", while "every contradiction has two sides".

There is a reason I mention this. Because it is so important. As a result of the revolutionary movement, countless working people, those who were "formerly apathetic", are now "politically active", "rising up", determined to "make some changes". It is those same workers, or at least the most advanced, "internationalist workers", who must become class conscious, raised to the level of true Marxists, Communists, at least in regards to "Party activity", according to Lenin.

This reference to a "Party", is that of a true Communist Party, which does not yet exist, at least here in North America. More on that subject, later on in this article.

The "activity" is a reference to giving direction to the revolutionary movement that is currently sweeping the country. For the moment- strictly for the moment! - it is merely spontaneous, lacking focus. It must become focused on overthrowing the bourgeoisie, smashing the existing state apparatus, and establishing a society of Scientific Socialism, through Council (Soviet) Power, and the Dictatorship of the Proletariat.

As the Russian word for Council is Soviet, it is as yet not clear, which word will become common place.

The precise name is incidental. The "members of the public", the "common people", the "rank and file", as that is the manner in which they refer to themselves, will make that decision.

No one, or at least no one "with a lick of sense", is about to dispute the fact that capitalism has reached a "state of crisis".

The national debt now stands at *thirty-four trillion,* and *rising.* The President is suffering from dementia. Mass murder is commonplace, drug overdoses are routine, the police are powerless, unemployment is widespread, countless people are hungry, as well as homeless, and the food banks are running out of food. The working people are "fed up", demanding change! And the government officials are focused on the upcoming *presidential election! Nero fiddled while Rome burned!*

What we have here is the very definition of a revolutionary situation.

As Lenin stated, in "Left Wing Communism, An Infantile Disorder", "For a revolution to take place, it is not enough for the exploited and oppressed masses to realize the impossibility of living in the old way, and demand changes; for a revolution to take place, it is essential that the exploiters should not be able to live and rule in the old way. It is only when the *'lower classes' do not want* to live in the old way, and the 'upper classes' *cannot carry on in the old way,* that the revolution can triumph". (italics by Lenin)

That is an accurate description of our current state of affairs!

Yet that is not enough. For a revolution to be *successful*, something more is needed.

That "something more" is the raising of the level of awareness of the working class. They must become "class conscious", aware of themselves as a class, complete with their own class interests. Or as Lenin stated, "A majority of the workers (or at least a majority of the class conscious, thinking and politically active workers) should fully realize that revolution is necessary, and that they should be prepared to die for it".

As yet, the "majority" of the most advanced workers, those who are "class conscious, thinking and politically active", have not reached that point. Not all of them are convinced of the "need for revolution", and all too many are not "prepared to die for it".

Our current situation is similar to that which existed in Russia, in the summer of 1917. The previous "March Revolution" had managed to overthrow Czar Nicholas, so that a democratic republic had been established, a "Provisional Government", led by Kerensky, under the control of the capitalists and landlords. The "common people", the workers and family farmers, referred to as peasants, had certain democratic rights, if only "on paper".

As is well known, Lenin returned from exile in April of that year. He was determined to carry the Russian revolution through to a proper conclusion, to Scientific Socialism, Soviet Power and the Dictatorship of the Proletariat. But *only when the workers and poor peasants were properly prepared!*

Shortly after his return, there was a "spontaneous uprising". This has gone down in history as the "Revolutionary July Days". This could have led to a full scale revolution, with the proletariat and poor peasants seizing power. It did not, as Lenin called for calm, a peaceful demonstration. There is a reason for this.

Lenin wrote an article, titled "The Eighteenth of June", concerning the "Revolutionary July Days". Within that article, there is one paragraph which I find to be of particular importance: "Let the people break with the policy of trust in the capitalists. Let them put their trust in the revolutionary class- the proletariat. The source of power lies in it, and only in it. It alone is the pledge that the interests of the *majority* will be served, the interests of the working and exploited people, who, though held down by war and capital, are capable of defeating war and capital!" (italics by Lenin)

This is to stress the fact that the *proletariat,* and *only* the *proletariat,* has the power to overthrow the bourgeoisie!

As Lenin also stated, in his article "Three Crises", "The vast majority of the country's population is petty bourgeois by its living conditions, and more so by its ideas…. There is an urban proletariat in this country, mature enough to go its own way, but not yet able to draw at once the majority of semi proletarians to its side".

This is to say that the level of awareness, the class consciousness, of the working class, the proletariat, was insufficient. Before a successful revolution could be mounted, the class consciousness, of the proletariat, had to be raised.

It was only when the "urban proletariat" was strong enough, sufficiently class conscious, to "draw at once the semi proletarians to its side", that the revolution could succeed.

From this, it is clear that our immediate goal is to raise the level of awareness, of the proletariat, in preparation for Scientific Socialism, in the form of Council Power and the Dictatorship of the Proletariat.

As for those who may object that this is a "tall order", I can only respond that you are right. Yet under far more difficult circumstances, Lenin was able to perform that very task. Within a few short months, the workers and poor peasants of Russia were able to mount the successful Great October Soviet Socialist Revolution.

By contrast, the majority of the American population is working class, proletarians, and quite well cultured. Most of them own, or at least have access to, digital devices. This makes it possible to raise their level of awareness, through the use of the internet.

No doubt, there are certain members of the middle class, who consider the election of Donald Trump, to be a matter of no concern. May I suggest that such people are either "not overly bright", or are "living in denial".

For those with a "modicum of intelligence", we should point out that your "days are numbered". Your "dream", that of joining the ranks of the billionaires, the bourgeoisie, is about to be shattered. All businesses but seven, and all banks but five, are *Too Small To Succeed!* Very soon, you are about to become financially ruined, forced into the ranks of the proletariat.

Even among the ranks of the bourgeois economists, the more astute can see the "writing on the wall". From the depths of bitterness and despair, they face the fact that Marx was right. They even "wave around" a copy of the Communist Manifesto, as if it is their very own personal "death certificate". And in a very real sense, it is!

They must be given credit, for at least having the honesty to face the fact that capitalism is failing. The stock market is about to "crash", and countless banks and businesses are about to go broke. The country is about to enter a Second Great Depression, even more severe than the First!

They must also be given credit for being men of action! Rather than "slashing their wrists", or just sitting back, waiting for the "axe to fall", they are preparing for the approaching financial collapse. In fact, they are "hoarding" valuable metals, in the form of gold and silver, placing them in Safety Deposit Boxes. As if that is going to do a "world of good"! It merely postpones the day that they will have to "enter the ranks" of the proletariat, to go "looking for a job"!

The problem is not Trump. He is merely a loud mouthed fool, a demagogue who has "visions" of crowning himself as Emperor, a stooge in the hands of the bourgeoisie.

The real problem is one of monopoly capitalism. The current ruling class of monopoly capitalists, the multi billionaires, the bourgeoisie, have to be overthrown. This can be accomplished *only* by the *working class*, the *proletariat*, the only truly consistent revolutionary class. Now they have to be made aware of this.

As previously stated, it is my opinion that the "key link" now, in the class struggle, is to raise the level of awareness of the working class. They must be prepared to overthrow the multi billionaires, the bourgeoisie, to smash the existing state apparatus, and replace it with *Council Power*, and the *Dictatorship of the Proletariat! Scientific Socialism!*

Perhaps we can best think of Trump as the "*immediate problem*", as that is precisely the case. In the process of stopping Trump, we can also raise the level of awareness of the working class.

Pressure must be applied, to the ruling class of multi billionaires. This necessarily involves the use of both legal and illegal methods.

Consider the legal methods. Experts on Constitutional law must challenge the 20-20 "presidential election", on the grounds that it was fraudulent, as it did not follow the procedure laid out in the Constitution, and in particular, the Twelfth Amendment. It follows that Biden is a fraudulent President, and Harris is a fraudulent Vice President. For that reason, they should be removed from office.

It is also a fact that Biden is a sick man, mentally ill, suffering from dementia. As he is incapable of making rational decisions, he should be removed from office, using the Constitution, and in particular, Section 4 of the Twenty Fifth Amendment.

Both of these proposed court challenges, must also be highly publicized. As this will attract the attention of countless working people, it can be used to raise the level of awareness of that class, the proletariat.

It is entirely possible that the attorneys, who are making those arguments, may well be "muzzled", placed under "gag orders", by the judges. For that reason, others, possibly Leftist "celebrities", preferably "movie stars", may be called upon to make the appropriate statements, to the press.

These "statements", by Leftist people, must include references to classes, and the conflict between the classes. It is best to use the popular terms, followed by the correct scientific terms. Such examples may include the "monopoly capitalists", the "multi billionaires", the "bourgeoisie", formerly referred to as the "one percent". The working class, the "common people", the "rank and file", are the "proletariat". It is necessary to overthrow the bourgeoisie, smash the existing state apparatus, and crush that class of parasites, under "Council Power", and the "Dictatorship of the Proletariat".

Working people pay strict attention to the opinion of "celebrities"! If "movie stars" are making this pitch, the level of awareness of countless members, of the working class, will be raised! These terms will soon become "household expressions". At that point, we will know that we are succeeding!

As well, social media must be "flooded" with such statements. We can only hope that they "go viral".

This brings us to illegal methods. The various Councils, which have sprung and are working in secret, have to redouble their efforts. It is essential that they get in touch with other Councils, as well as with "groups of internationalist workers", and prepare for the Insurrection. At the same time, the leaders of those Councils, along with the most advanced "internationalist workers", must create a true Communist Party, one which calls for the Dictatorship of the Proletariat. As I have covered this in previous articles, there is no need to repeat it here.

Allow me to reassure all middle class people, including those who are considered to be "upper" middle class, possibly with assets of tens or even hundreds of millions: Communists are not the enemy! The enemy is the bourgeoisie. They have decided to ruin you. Unless, of course, you have assets of at least a billion dollars! Not many people do!

For all others, the skills you have learned, under capitalism, will be in demand, under Scientific Socialism. You will receive the respect that you deserve, and will be paid accordingly.

As regards the class of people, the bourgeoisie, who are determined to ruin you, feel free to embrace the age old adage: "Better to get even, than to get mad"!

Believe me when I say that, the science books are filled with distortions and outright lies. Very soon, common people will locate several huge animals, which I have identified, using the directions I have provided.

The books of social science, as taught in University, merely *distort* the revolutionary theories of Marx and Lenin. Feel free to read the essential works, of those two great revolutionaries, with an open mind. Then bring that class awareness, to the proletariat.

Bear in mind that Trump is now being "fast tracked" for the White House. Further bear in mind that "Project 2025" is now set to be implemented.

There is no need to wait, for the revolution to spontaneously break out, into open class warfare. In October of 1917, Lenin took action, in order to prevent a "catastrophe".

That catastrophe was the plan of Kerensky, to surrender the capital of Petrograd, as a means of forestalling the Russian revolution.

In much the same manner, the plan of the American bourgeoisie, is to set up Trump as a figurehead President, soon to be Dictator, in order to forestall the American revolution. For that reason, an insurrection is required, before Trump is sworn into office. Otherwise, our task will indeed be a "hundred times more difficult".

Perhaps another slogan is appropriate:

Prepare For Insurrection!

CHAPTER 10

ELECTION OF FRENCH PARLIAMENT

France! The country in which, "more than anywhere else, the historical class struggles were each time fought out to a decision", according to Engels. Once again, the class struggles of France are being "fought out to a decision"!

This country is currently "making headlines". It has a "multi party" political system, in that there are so many political parties, there is almost no chance that any single party could win a majority of seats, in the French Parliament. For that reason, a coalition government is almost always necessary. The latest Parliamentary election, has proven to be no exception.

Incidentally, the Parliamentary Election is separate from the Presidential Election, which is held once every five years.

Recently, French President Macron decided to call a "snap" election, for the Parliament. It was widely anticipated that the National Rally Party, RN, led by Marine Le Pen, would "top the polls", win the most seats. The RN is considered to be a "Far Right" Party, so that it was expected that France was about to "move to the Right".

Precisely the opposite happened! France "moved to the Left"!

Immediately after President Macron called for this "snap election", several "Leftist" parties came together, the "Socialists", "Greens", "Communists" and "France Unbowed", to form that which they refer to as the "New Popular Front", NFP. The French press is referring to this merger as a "Far Left Coalition".

With the "Left" united, they were able to mount a solid defence, against the forces of the "Right". In the "first round" of voting, of the 577 elections for each of the constituencies, only 76 received the necessary fifty percent required, to be elected to Parliament. All the others had to proceed to a "second round" of voting.

In the second round of voting, it is customary for the three candidates, who won the most votes in the first round, to run against each other. Yet as the Left was united, one of the two Leftist candidates would withdraw from the race, so that the Leftist vote was not split. In this way, the voters got to choose between a Leftist candidate, and a "Right Wing" candidate. In this way, it was frequently the Leftist candidate, who won the election.

This serves as a fine example of Leftist candidates putting aside their differences, and uniting against a common enemy. In this way, the "United Left" managed to stop a "Far Right" party, from coming to power.

We can compare this to the second Russian revolution of 1917, the Great October Soviet Socialist Revolution. Lenin and the Bolsheviks did not immediately take undivided power. On the contrary, they made certain compromises, with another "Leftist"

Party, the Left Socialist Revolutionaries, and succeeded in forming a coalition government.

Now in France, Parliament is divided into "three big groups", each deeply divided, those who have "no tradition of working together", according to the press.

The self-described leader of the NFP is Jean-Luc Melenchon. He is calling for the resignation of Prime Minister Gabriel Attal, and wants President Macron to allow the NFP to govern.

Yet it is not that simple! As there are 577 seats in Parliament, a majority of 289 is required. The NFP won the most seats at 178, so that they require support of other parties, in order to form a government. The two other "big groups" of parties, are not at all anxious to work with the NFP. Parliament is in a state of gridlock!

As can be well expected, the French mainstream press is of the opinion that the "Far Right" has been "robbed". They think that the RN Party should have won, and that Marine Le Pen should be Prime Minister.

They are also of the opinion that we can expect an "extended period of political limbo". This on the "eve of a NATO summit"! And a mere "three weeks before the Paris Olympics"! Now France is "in chaos"!

The press is correct in referring to the situation in France as "chaotic", that there is "deep discontent". Numerous demonstrations are taking place, with Palestinian flags being waved. Far more so than French flags! Then there are the red flags, which may stand for revolution. As well, there are signs which openly call for "revolution".

As yet, there are no signs or slogans which contain class content. It is clear that the French proletariat is not yet class conscious.

The streets of France have been described as a "war zone", with "wide spread riots". "Left" and "Right" supporters are clashing, with masked demonstrators running through the streets, lighting flares and fighting with police. There have even been reports of the use of "Molotov Cocktails", flaming bottles of gasoline being thrown. If true, then that is an indication of a full blown revolution.

The journalists are also correct, when they say that the "political instability" within the country, can "have an impact outside the country", as France "plays a key role on the European and global stage". A revolution in France, is almost certain to spread to neighboring countries!

Without doubt, it is not just in America that the "ruling class can no longer rule in the old way", and has to "change their method of rule". It is also true in France. As well, the "lower classes", within France, are no longer "content to be ruled in the old way". In both countries, conditions are set for a successful socialist revolution.

It is also a fact that the country suffers from the lack of a true Communist Party, one which calls for Council Power, and the Dictatorship of the Proletariat. The French Communist Party is Communist in name only.

The advice given, in my previous article, applies also to the French proletariat, so there is no need to repeat it here.

The French revolution is bound to spread to neighboring countries, in Europe and possibly beyond. As well, the American revolution is bound to spread across North America, and possibly beyond. Truly, the world socialist revolution, as foreseen by Lenin, is within sight.

CHAPTER 11

SIGNIFICANCE OF NEW POPULAR FRONT

The latest Parliamentary election of France, has given rise to three "political bloks", within Parliament, technically referred to as the "National Assembly". Each "blok" is composed of a number of parties. This is necessary, as there are a great many political parties, within the country.

The mainstream press refers to these bloks as "Far Right", "Centrist", and "Far Left". This is their way of avoiding any mention of class terms.

As the people of Europe are supremely well aware of the existence of classes, this is rather strange. After all, the European class of people, referred to as the "nobility", are wide spread. The French are exceptional, in that they have dealt with their nobility in the Great French Revolution of 1789, so that they no longer exist, at least in France.

By contrast, in America, it is customary to deny the existence of classes. As the current French revolutionary uprising is "making headlines", we can use this to raise the level of awareness of the American working class, the proletariat. They have to be made aware of themselves, as a class, with their own class interests, which are diametrically opposed to the interests of the ruling class of multi billionaires, the bourgeoisie.

We should mention that four political parties came together, to form a "Leftist Coalition", or 'Bloc'. These Parties are the "Socialists", "Greens", "Communists", and "France Unbowed". This Bloc is referred to as the "New Popular Front", or "NFP". The mainstream press tends to refer to this Coalition as the "Far Left".

This Leftist Coalition was formed in response to the National Rally Coalition, RN, a "Far Right" coalition, which was widely expected to win the election. Yet the NFP won, as the Leftist parties were able to put aside their differences, and unite against a common enemy. As all trade union members are well aware, there is strength in numbers!

For the benefit of those who are just now becoming politically active, we should clarify that a "popular front" is defined as "any coalition of working-class and middle-class parties, including liberal and social democratic ones, united for the defense of democratic forms, against a presumed Fascist assault".

The New Popular Front is no exception to this rule. Their political platform includes raising the tax rate upon the wealthiest, to ninety percent, increasing the minimum wage, reducing the retirement age to sixty, and freezing the price of basic food items and energy.

Paltry reforms! The working class needs something more than reforms! The working class needs Revolution! Scientific

Socialism! Soviet Power and the Dictatorship of the Proletariat! The working class needs a true Communist Party!

Yet this victory, of the NFP, served to "strengthen and further" the revolutionary motion, as was predicted by Marx. The demonstrations are becoming ever more fierce, as the working people rise up.

Now the mainstream press is openly expressing fear of a French Civil War. They are careful to avoid the "R word", that of Revolution.

From the slogans and posters, of the French "protesters", it is clear that their level of awareness, is at about the same level as that of their American comrades. As both countries are close to revolutionary war, that is completely unacceptable.

It is also clear that Marxists, true Communists, those who call for Soviet Power the Dictatorship of the Proletariat, are either negligent, or nonexistent.

As that is the case, it is up to the working class, the proletariat, of both France and America, to raise their own level of awareness. More accurately, the most advanced workers must read the essential works of Marx and Lenin. These include the Communist Manifesto, State and Revolution, What Is To Be Done? Imperialism, the Highest Stage of Capitalism, and Left Wing Communism, An Infantile Disorder.

A proper understanding of those revolutionary works, will provide those workers with the information they need. They in turn, will lead the less advanced workers.

I refer to this as "removing the blindfold from the working people". As the proletariat is not class conscious, not aware of itself as a class, the class struggle can be compared to a match between two boxers, one of whom is blindfolded, swinging wildly in all directions. Every so often, he may land a "lucky punch", but purely by chance.

Of course, in my over simplified comparison, it is the proletariat who is blindfolded, in its boxing match with the monopoly capitalists. They are not aware that it is a class struggle, the proletariat against the bourgeoisie. Rest assured, the bourgeoisie is well aware of itself, as a class, with its own class interests. Those interests come at the expense of the proletariat!

As France has no true Communist Party, one which calls for the Dictatorship of the Proletariat, the most advanced, or "internationalist workers", will come together to form "groups", according to Lenin. It is these groups of internationalist workers who can study these revolutionary works, thus raising their level of awareness.

In this way, they will learn that the state apparatus, which has been set up by the capitalists, for the sole purpose of crushing the "lower classes", must be smashed, at the time of the revolution, and replaced with another state apparatus, in the form of the Dictatorship of the Proletariat. This is necessary, in order to crush the bourgeoisie, as they make every effort to "restore their paradise lost".

It is also very likely that Councils, or Soviets, or "Sovietiques", as I believe that is the correct French word, have taken shape. Revolutionary motion frequently gives rise to such working class organizations. It is further very likely that they are currently working "underground", keeping a "low profile", as the work they are doing is illegal.

To the leaders of those Sovietiques, may I suggest that you focus your efforts. Prepare for revolution and the subsequent

Dictatorship of the Proletariat. In other words, prepare for Insurrection!

The most advanced workers must be trained, in preparation for that Insurrection. Their level of awareness must be raised, to the level of Communists, at least in regard to Party activity. After all, soon they will be placed in positions of authority, after the revolution, so that any training they receive now, will prove to be most valuable.

As well, get in touch with other Sovietiques, possibly through the internet. Be discrete. Do not make it easy for the government authorities. Remember what happened to the workers of the Paris Commune!

No doubt, many of you have been to university, and been exposed to the revolutionary theories of Marx and Lenin. That places you in a better position to take part in the creation of a true Communist Party. There is an urgent need for such a Party. The most advanced workers can assist you with this.

The French working class, the proletariat, is currently leading the revolutionary movement in Western Europe. Or at least, they are playing a leading role. For that reason, we can expect other countries to follow that lead. Without doubt, a great many countries, within Europe and beyond, are about to experience a revolution.

Now it is up to Marxists, Scientific Socialists, Communists, to give that Revolution the proper direction. We will know we are succeeding, when the posters and slogans proclaim:

Scientific Socialism!
Dictatorship of the Proletariat!
Soviet Power!
Workers of the World, Unite!

CHAPTER 12

REPUBLICAN NATIONAL CONVENTION, 2024

After many months of speculation, the RNC has just confirmed that which everybody knew. Donald Trump is now the official Republican candidate for the Presidency. He also chose a "running mate", for the office of Vice President, that of Senator Vance.

Now it is up to the Democratic National Convention to select a candidate for the Presidency, as well as a suitable "running mate", for the office of Vice President.

At that point, the voters will get to choose which candidates, from one of the two Parties, will go to Washington in January, and be sworn into office. All of which is completely *Unconstitutional! In direct violation of the Twelfth Amendment!*

As I have earlier copied that Amendment, there is no need to repeat it here. I can only repeat that the Twelfth Amendment lays out the procedure to be followed, in all *federal elections!* There is no mention of any *presidential election!* Nor is there any mention of any "running mate". For that matter, there is no mention of any *political party!* There is no mention of any "November Election"! There is no *"President Elect"! The American voters have nothing to say, concerning the federal election!*

By *Constitutional Law,* it is the *Electors, and only the Electors,* who are appointed *by the states, and only by the states,* who get to vote for the President, on one ballot, and on a separate ballot, vote for the Vice President. The Electors vote for the individuals of *their choice!* The states have no right to *meddle in a federal election!*

This is my less than subtle way of pointing out, that this "presidential election", currently under way, is *fraudulent!* It is in direct *violation of the Constitution!* Just as the 2020 "presidential election" was *fraudulent!* Which means that Biden is a *fraudulent President,* and Harris is a *fraudulent Vice President!* Just as *every President,* and *every Vice President,* elected since the days of the Civil War, have been *fraudulent!*

Naturally, the mainstream press is focused on the Convention. They are mainly talking about Trump, and his "running mate". As if the Republican presidential candidate has the legal right to choose the Vice Presidential candidate! He has no such right!

That being said, it is encouraging to see the protesters, demonstrating in the streets of Milwaukee, outside the "closed doors" of the RNC. It is the "Leftist press" which is covering these protests, posting this on the internet.

Several thousand people have showed up, forming a coalition of as many as *one hundred* "activist groups". They are clearly a mixture of young and old, students and seniors, veterans and "newbies", male and female, of various ethnic groups. From the signs they are carrying, it is clear that they have a broad list of demands, including that of "immigration rights", "reproductive rights" and "LGBTQ" rights. As well, many signs are in support of the "People of Palestine". They call for an "End to US aid to Israel", and "Support for People of Gaza". This is in addition to the countless "Stop Trump" signs.

Perhaps the most encouraging sign said: "No War But Class War! Fight For Communism!" At least it mentioned "Class War"!

Even more encouraging is the fact that, for the last two years, this Coalition has been "taking the city to court", to get permits to demonstrate "as close as possible to the RNC".

The Coalition has been *pursuing court action* for two years! Excellent! Now it is time for the Coalition to become *focused!* Now is *not* the time for *half measures!* Now is the time to "pursue court action" *against the fraudulent 2024 federal election!*

As I have documented this in a previous article, there is no need to go into it in detail. I can only summarize that Biden is suffering from dementia, and has to be removed from office, if only under the Twenty Fifth Amendment. As well, both Biden and Harris were sworn into office, under a fraudulent system. They must be removed.

Without doubt, "court action" is required, in order to prevent another fraudulent "2024 Presidential Election". As middle class attorney's have already initiated "court action", in the city of Milwaukee, it is clear that they are prepared to take legal action. The only difference is that the next "court action" must involve federal courts.

Bear in mind that the main thing is to raise the level of awareness of the working class, the proletariat. These public court challenges should serve that purpose. Any ruling, in favor of these challenges, can only be viewed as a bonus.

The American voters- who have no legal voice in this federal election! - are being presented with the choice of two men for the office of President. One is suffering from dementia, and the other is an accomplished liar, a true psycho.

Project 2025 has been completed. Now it is just a little matter of swearing in Trump, as President. The first step towards setting him up as Dictator. The man must be stopped. These proposed court actions may help to serve that purpose.

Otherwise, our tasks will be a hundred times more difficult.

CHAPTER 13

KAMELA HARRIS RUNNING FOR PRESIDENT

President Joe Biden just made it "perfectly clear" that he is running for re-election, and has no intention of "stepping down", according to the "mainstream" press. The "Leftist" press is of the opinion that there are only two people who want Joe Biden to run for President. Those two people are Joe Biden and Donald Trump.

The real "power players" in Washington, those who work "behind the scenes", and "call the shots", are of a different opinion. They told Biden to call a press conference and announce that he is not running for re-election, but that he is "passing the torch" to "his" Vice President, Kamela Harris. So he did.

Now the press is counting down the days until the Democratic National Convention, to be held in Chicago, on August 19. On that day, it is widely anticipated that Kamela Harris will be "crowned" as the Presidential candidate, for the Democratic

Party. Then again, there are two "Ladies in Waiting", both former "First Ladies", who would love to "Steal the Crown".

This in no way changes the fact that "buying the Presidency", is most expensive. It costs billions of dollars! The candidate for President, for either Party, must get the support of those with "deep pockets", who are prepared to invest the billions required. Of course, those "deep pocket people" expect a "proper return" on their "invested capital". In popular terms, the individual elected as President, is "in the pocket" of some very rich people, multi billionaires, one and all.

Perhaps it would be best if those multi billionaires, members of the class of people whom are referred to as the bourgeoisie, were to be "relieved of this burden". After all, they no doubt have their hands full, between manipulating the stock market, avoiding paying taxes and "preserving the light of humanity", by "sending people to Mars". Such visionaries should not stoop to concern themselves with mundane matters, such as "Presidential Elections".

All joking aside, the multi billionaires have just "tipped their hand", to put this in popular terms. They have decided to offer voters a choice, between Trump and Harris. Even though the voters have nothing to say about this!

There is an urgent need to expose the hypocrisy, of the ruling class of bourgeoisie. As previously stated, the Twelfth Amendment to the Constitution, documents the procedure to be followed in all *federal elections!* There is *no presidential election!* The November vote is *Unconstitutional!* It is the *Electors,* and *only the Electors,* who are appointed *by the states,* and *only by the states,* who have the legal right to vote for the individual, *of their choice,* for President. They also have the legal right to vote, *on a separate ballot,* for the individual, *of their choice,* for Vice President. The states have *no right* to meddle in a federal election!

The members of the working class, the proletariat, must be made aware of this. In this way, their level of awareness will be raised. They must be made aware of themselves, as a class, with their own class interests. This will help to prepare them for the approaching Insurrection, and the subsequent Dictatorship of the Proletariat.

The "common people", as the members of the working class refer to themselves, are paying strict attention to the "Presidential Election", as the mainstream press refers to it. For that reason, it can be used to raise their level of awareness.

As for those who may object, quite reasonably, that challenging **these** "Presidential Elections" in court, as Unconstitutional, is expensive, I can only respond that you are so right. Allow me to add that *not challenging* these "Presidential Elections", in court, is far more expensive!

As I have previously documented, the bourgeoisie has recently "laid down the law". *All businesses,* as well as *all banks,* with "assets" of less than *half a trillion,* are *Too Small To Succeed!* Even General Motors is *Too Small To Succeed!*

All "small businesses", with assets of *less than half a trillion,* are about to go broke! Those assets are about to be picked up by the multi billionaires.

Regardless of the results of the next federal election, all small business owners are about to lose everything. The "upper class", the bourgeoisie, has decided to wipe out the middle class. The only revolutionary class that can stop them, is the proletariat.

They in turn, need to be prepared. They need to become class conscious.

Time is not on our side. America is a "powder keg", so that any "spark" could cause an "explosion", an "Insurrection". As well, Western Europe is in "turmoil", to use the stilted expression of the mainstream press. Various countries, including France, Germany and Great Britain, are close to full revolution.

Very recently, the country of Bangladash, in South Asia, has been "making headlines". As it has a population of 174 million people, and a sizeable working class, it is a country that is not to be underestimated. The press is reporting that the situation has deteriorated, to a state of "civil war". Certainly, the students are in revolt, and a prison has been "stormed", with 800 inmates being released. That is certainly an indication of full scale revolution. The experience of previous revolutions tells us that it will very likely spread to neighbouring countries, such as India, Russia and China.

Worldwide revolution! The World Socialist Republic, as predicted by Lenin, is on the horizon. Now it is up to us to prepare, for the Insurrection, and the subsequent Dictatorship of the Proletariat. The alternative is not to be considered.

CHAPTER 14

INTERNATIONAL WAR CRIMINAL ADDRESSES CONGRESS

The Prime Minister of Israel, an individual who is wanted by the International Criminal Court, to face charges of war crimes, just addressed a "Joint Session of Congress". This is to say that the House of Representatives, as well as the Senate, got together to hear Benjamin Netanyahu.

The leaders of both political parties, Democratic and Republican, of both "Houses of Congress", invited this individual to speak.

The Republican Members, of both the House and the Senate, appeared to be wildly enthusiastic. Netanyahu was first met with a rousing applause, and during his speech, was frequently interrupted by "standing ovations".

The Democratic Members were somewhat more subdued. Even though the Democratic leaders had invited Netanyahu, over a hundred Democratic "lawmakers", refused to attend. As well, one House Member, the only Palestinian American in Congress, held a sign with "War Criminal" on one side, and "Guilty of Genocide" on the other.

Outside that building, on the streets of Washington, tens of thousands of protesters, from all across the country, were expressing their opposition. Many of them represented an organization called "Jewish Voice for Peace". Among them, were over a dozen rabbis. All were wearing T shirts that said "Not In Our Name", and "Stop Arming Israel". As well, their signs proclaimed, "Jews say: Stop the Genocide", and "No More Weapons to Israel", and "Anti-Israel Is Not Anti-Semitism". A great many of these Jewish protesters were arrested.

Of course, numerous other organizations were represented, in the protests, including several "major unions". This too, is of great significance, as it is an indication of the breadth and depth of the revolutionary motion.

Naturally, Netanyahu slandered these patriotic citizens, who were exercising their democratic right to protest. He accused them of being "in the service" of a foreign power, of being "Irans useful idiots".

The protesters were a broad mixture of people, young and old, male and female, of various ethnic backgrounds, all opposed to the genocide being committed against the people of Palestine. They are especially determined to stop the American government from providing any more weapons to Israel, as these weapons are being used against Palestinian civilians.

In their attempt to get closer to the government buildings, in which Netanyahu was speaking, the protesters came into conflict with the police. For that reason, countless people were "pepper sprayed", and many others were arrested.

Possibly the finest coverage of this protest, was by a journalist from TRT, Turkish Radio and Television. His article was titled the "Corruption of American Political Power", by "Pro War Billionaires". As he stated: "That billionaire class is the reason why Netanyahu is being invited here…because of the corruption of American politics by pro war billionaires, who essentially control both Parties, and control Kamala Harris, Joe Biden, and Donald Trump, who is set to meet with Netanyahu at Mar-a-Lago on Friday. The pro war billionaire class is the reason Netanyahu was invited to US."

Although the article suffers from a number of defects, that is incidental to the fact that the author makes reference to the existence of classes. That is precisely what is needed, in order to raise the level of awareness of the working class, the proletariat.

He could well have added that the 'billionaire class" is technically referred to as the "bourgeoisie". He is also correct in pointing out that the "billionaire class" is "pro war", is responsible for the "corruption of American politics", has "control of both Parties", both Democratic and Republican, as well as control of the President and Vice President.

True, he did not state it quite this clearly, but he documented it, and that is the important thing. We can only hope that other "Leftist" journalists will "follow suit", and start to report the news properly, in class terms.

Indeed, all high ranking politicians are "in the pocket" of the bourgeoisie, the multi billionaires. It can hardly be otherwise, as the election of the President, as well as the Vice President, costs many *billions of dollars*. The multi billionaires finance the election campaigns of these candidates, of both Parties, and once elected, those same politicians are indebted to the multi billionaires! Both Parties serve the same class! The bourgeoisie!

The 2024 federal election is scheduled to be no different. The voters will be allowed to choose between the candidates of the two Parties. The Republicans are offering Trump, for the office of President, with Pence as his "running mate", for the office of Vice President. The Democrats will almost certainly select Kamala Harris, for the office of President, with the candidate of her choice, her "running mate", for the office of Vice President. All of which is completely *Unconstitutional!*

Yet this will almost certainly take place, *unless the political parties are forced to abide by the Constitution!*

Of course, I am referring to the Twelfth Amendment to the Constitution, which lays out the procedure to be followed, in all *federal elections!* As I have documented in previous articles, the American voters have nothing to say, concerning the election of the President, or the Vice President. By *Constitutional law!*

There is no need to repeat it here. I will merely point out that the "Two Party System" is completely Unconstitutional! It has been established, by the multi billionaires, the bourgeoisie, as a convenient method of rule. Under this system, anyone who wants to become President, must first secure many billions of dollars. In the process, they become indebted to those same multi billionaires, the bourgeoisie.

A court order is required to force a *legal* federal election. This will *not* have the effect of overthrowing the bourgeoisie. It *will* have the effect of *raising the level of awareness* of the working class, the proletariat.

The revolutionary motion is growing ever stronger. The fact that so many people, of so many different walks of life, as well as the labor unions, are protesting, is a reliable indication of this.

We have no way of knowing which "spark" will ignite a full scale revolution. It could happen any day. It will result in the overthrow of the bourgeoisie, the smashing of the existing state apparatus, and the establishment of the Dictatorship of the Proletariat. The more prepared we are, the smoother will be the transition.

Also as previously mentioned, it is only middle class attorneys, those who are experts on Constitutional law, who can challenge the federal elections, in a court of law. This is well worth the effort, the time and money.

It may help to think of this as a "future investment". An alliance is required, of the middle class, the petty bourgeois, with the working class, the proletariat, against the ruling class of multi billionaires, the bourgeoisie.

Middle class people have nothing to lose, as the bourgeoisie has recently announced their intention of destroying the middle class. They are not joking.

Nor are we joking. Those of us who are Scientific Socialists, Communists, are offering middle class people an alternative. Join us in establishing the Dictatorship of the Proletariat. Your training and skills will be in demand, under Socialism. Those who cooperate, will be respected and rewarded. Those who oppose us, will be treated in the same manner as the members of the bourgeoisie, the parasites who have no useful skills. The experience will not be pleasant.

Bear in mind that both Marx and Lenin were middle class intellectuals. Feel free to proudly follow in their footsteps. Join the revolutionary class of the proletariat, the class that "holds the future in its hands". You will not be disappointed.

CHAPTER 15

TRUMP DOUBLES DOWN ON DICTATOR

onald Trump recently gave a campaign speech, in West Palm Beach, Florida, in which he did something highly unusual, completely unexpected, and rather strange. Trump broke with his long standing tradition of "speaking lies, only lies, and nothing but lies". Remarkably enough -even though his lips were moving! - he actually spoke the truth! This is what he said:

"You have to get out and vote. You won't have to do it anymore. Four years, it will be fixed. You won't have to vote anymore. In four years, you won't have to vote again".

We can only express our most sincere, heartfelt gratitude to this former President, and current candidate for the office of President, this multi billionaire, this monopoly capitalist, this

member of the class of people, referred to as the bourgeoisie. Trump has just "tipped his hand", revealed his plan to set himself up as "Dictator, on Day One", so that American voters will be "relieved of the burden" of voting! But first they have to "get out and vote", just "one more time"!

That "one more time" is a reference to the upcoming "November vote", the "popular vote for the Presidency". A vote which is completely *fraudulent! Unconstitutional!*

It is to the credit of a certain "Leftist" journalist, that he "broke this story". It is available, on the internet, under the title "President Trump Casts Vision for '24 And Beyond".

As this Leftist journalist pointed out, if Trump wins the 2024 "Presidential election", he will "set himself up as "Dictator On Day One", deport immigrants en masse, strip citizenship from those who burn flags, which falls under the First Amendment right to free speech… Donald Trump will end our democracy if he gets back into power".

For purposes of clarification, we should mention that there is no law against burning the American flag, as long as it belongs to the individual. Yet it should be discouraged, out of respect for the working people, patriotic Americans, many of whom have fought under that flag. We do not want to offend them.

Another Leftist journalist, one with a strong sense of democracy, produced a video, titled "Top Republicans Just Turned On Trump…Then Buried Him!"

In this video, he gave credit to the former Vice President, Mike Pence. Even though he was hardly a fan of Pence, he pointed out that Pence took a principled stand. He refused to "falsify the results of the 2020 Presidential election", according to the journalist.

As Pence is reported to have said, "Anyone who puts themselves over the Constitution, should never be President of the United States".

As the journalist pointed out, "We are all pro-democracy, we all believe the Constitution needs to be upheld. ...Trump tried to steal our last election. There is no greater threat to our Republic. He resorted to lies and violence to keep himself in power. There was no evidence of election fraud".

Except that there was election fraud! Not the fraud that Trump was referring to, but fraud nonetheless. As the 2020 "Presidential election" did not follow the procedure laid out in the Twelfth Amendment, it was clearly fraudulent.

Still another Leftist journalist produced another fine video, titled "Police Raid Library to Enforce Book Bans: Is Fascism Already Here?"

In this video, the journalist pointed out that, in the state of Texas, the police are "raiding libraries", in order to enforce "book bans". It is apparently a "crime" in Texas to "pass out certain books". The legal guidelines are "rather vague", but include "books that make people feel bad about race", as well as "any reference to a gay character".

This journalist pointed out that "This is the way the Nazis started. Book burning! First they come for the books. Librarians. Teachers. New fascist groups. All over social media. This is fascism".

This journalist certainly has good reason to be concerned. It is true that in Germany, the Nazis, fascists one and all, started by burning books. Yet book burning, by itself, is not necessarily fascist. It could well be reactionary.

This "begs the question". What is the difference between fascist and reactionary?

According to the internet, a fascist is "A far right form of government, in which most of the country's power is held by one ruler, or a small group, under a single party. Fascist governments are usually totalitarian and authoritarian one party states".

Also according to the internet, a reactionary is defined as "opposing social or political liberalization or reform". From this, it is clear that all fascists are reactionary, but not all reactionaries are fascists.

Lenin goes into this in his excellent work, Imperialism, the Highest Stage of Capitalism:

"The question as to whether it is possible to reform the basis of imperialism, whether to go forward to the aggravation of the antagonisms which it engenders, or backwards, towards allaying these antagonisms, is a fundamental question in the critique of imperialism. As a consequence of the fact that the political features of imperialism are *reaction all along the line,* and increased national oppression, resulting from the oppression of the financial oligarchy and the elimination of free competition, a democratic petty bourgeois opposition has been rising against imperialism in almost all imperialist countries, since the beginning of the twentieth century". (my italics)

May I suggest that we are experiencing "reaction all along the line", in the form of "book burning", which is not necessarily fascism. May I further suggest "going forward to the aggravation of the antagonisms which imperialism engenders", by challenging the legality of the "Presidential election", in a federal court of law.

The alternative, that of "reforming the basis of imperialism", possibly by supporting the presumptive Democratic Party candidate for President, Kamala Harris, can best be described as a "petty bourgeois opposition", one which has no chance of success. After all, the bourgeoisie has recently announced that it plans to wipe out the middle class. Now is not the time for "half measures". The election of Harris, to the Presidency, will change nothing.

The previous examples, of videos produced by concerned Leftist journalists, indicate that there are a great many middle class people, who are deeply concerned. Now is the time to unite all Leftist opposition, both middle class and working class, in a legal challenge to the federal elections.

Such a court challenge will help to raise the level of awareness of the working class, the proletariat. They must be prepared for the approaching revolution, the insurrection, the smashing of the existing state apparatus, and the establishment of Scientific Socialism, in the form of the Dictatorship of the Proletariat.

As the proletariat is the only consistently revolutionary class, the "class that holds the future in its hands", that is the "way forward".

CHAPTER 16

STATEMENT IN SUPPORT OF THE REVOLUTIONARY UPRISING IN VENEZUELA

Venezuela is a South American country of possibly thirty million people, and quite highly industrialized. The main industries are oil, mining and steel. There are not a great many family farmers, referred to as peasants. This means that there is a high percentage of workers, proletarians.

As it is located in South America, it is considered to be a "Latin American" country, in that the official language is Spanish. In fact, all countries of South America are considered to be Latin American. For that reason, people from such countries are referred to as "Latinos".

Incidentally, the word "Latino" comes from the fact that Latin gave rise to various "Romance" languages. These include Spanish, French, Italian, Portuguese and Romanian. Yet the expression "Latino" is generally restricted to Spanish speaking people from South America.

GERALD McISAAC

A Presidential election was recently held in Venezuela. President Nicholas Maduro is claiming victory, even though the opposition, led by Maria Machado, says that Edmundo Gonzales won the election, in a "landslide victory".

The political party of Maduro, refers to itself as the Partido Socialista Unido de Venezuela, PSUV, or in English, the United Socialist Party of Venezuela.

Regardless of the fact that they refer to themselves as "Socialist", they are anything but Socialist! They are supremely "right wing", completely reactionary. It is important to bear in mind that any political party can refer to itself as "Socialist". The only requirement is the ability to spell the word!

Since the vote, there have been widespread protests. The mainstream press is reporting that "Venezuela is on the brink of collapse", that "there is chaos in the streets", that "the country is in the midst of a popular uprising".

Without doubt, the country is experiencing a "mass movement", or a "revolutionary uprising", to phrase it in scientific terms. Most common people think that the election was "rigged", that Maduro "stole the election", that Gonzalez was the "real winner". This has given rise to "violent demonstrations", with protesters chanting such slogans as **"Out the Dictator!"**, and "Long Live Freedom!".

It is clear that the "common people" of Venezuela, both workers and family farmers, are determined to secure their democratic right to elect the leaders of their choice, through free, fair and independent elections.

This is most encouraging, as according to Engels, "Universal suffrage is an index of the maturity of the working class. It cannot, and never will be, anything more in the modern state".

This "spontaneous mass movement", these protests against a "stolen election", is an indication that the Venezuelan working class is "quite mature".

Further, according to Lenin, "The omnipotence of 'wealth' is thus more *secure* in a democratic republic, since it does not depend on the faulty political shell of capitalism. A democratic republic is the best possible political shell for capitalism, and therefore, once capital has gained control of this very best shell… it established its power so securely, so firmly, that *no* change, either of persons, of institutions, or of parties in the bourgeois democratic republic, can shake it". (italics by Lenin)

This is to say that, even if the protesters succeed in securing a new, democratically elected President, complete with a different Party, nothing will change! The monopoly capitalist class, the bourgeoisie, will still be in charge! Now it is a matter of making the working class, the proletariat, aware of this!

President Maduro has responded to these protests with a display of brute force. He has ordered the police and military to "crush the attempt of the far right to seize power". This despite the fact that Maduro represents the "far right"! He has also ordered the arrest of "opposition leaders".

For that reason, Maria Machado has gone "into hiding", in fear for her life. She has also called for "nationwide protests", to be held on Saturday.

The journalists have conducted interviews with numerous protesters. As a result, they are convinced that these protests are "different from previous protests", in that the common people are "fed up", that they are "determined to enact change". As the protesters phrase it, "enough is enough"!

Perhaps we can compare this situation, in Venezuela, to that of Russia, in the spring of 1917.

In February of that year, the Russian Czar, or Emperor, had been overthrown, and a democratic republic established, with Kerensky as the leader. The common people, workers and family farmers, had some democratic rights, if only on paper. This made it possible for Lenin to return from exile, in April of that year.

As I have documented, in previous writings, he found a "dual power" in place. The state power, of the Kerensky regime, was being challenged, by the state power of the "Soviets"- or "Sovietica" in Spanish- of the working people!

The fact is that revolutionary motion frequently- but by no means always! - gives rise to Soviets. These are also referred to as Councils, in English. For the purposes of this article, I will refer to them as Soviets.

It is very likely that Soviets have also made an appearance in Venezuela, as a result of that revolutionary motion. Assuming that is the case, then they are the nucleus of a new, proletarian state power. It is up to the Venezuelan Soviets to unite, to overthrow the corrupt capitalist regime of Maduro, smash the existing state apparatus, and establish a state of Scientific Socialism, in the form of the Dictatorship of the Proletariat.

But first it is necessary to raise the level of awareness of the common people, especially the working class, the proletariat. They must become "class conscious", aware of themselves as a class, complete with their own class interests. The conditions of life, of the working class, do not lead to this awareness.

For that reason, it is up to middle class intellectuals to bring that awareness to the proletariat. It is only the middle class which is aware of the revolutionary theories of Marx and Lenin, as those theories are taught only in Universities, and then only with a view to distorting those same theories.

This is the duty of a true Communist Party, but it is doubtful that such a Communist Party exists in Venezuela. Bear in mind that the Dictatorship of the Proletariat is the "touchstone" of a true Communist Party, according to Lenin.

In the absence of a Communist Party, those whom Lenin refers to as "internationalist workers", will come together. To such groups of advanced workers, I can only suggest a careful reading of State and Revolution, by Lenin.

Bear in mind that in the summer of 1917, as the Russian Revolution was gaining strength, the Russian officials, under Kerensky, determined to kill Lenin. For that reason, he went into hiding, and prepared for the Russian Revolution. In anticipation of the Insurrection, he wrote State and Revolution.

That article lays out the procedure to be followed, in order to conduct a successful revolution. At the time of the Insurrection, the government must be overthrown, the existing state apparatus must be smashed, and replaced with a new and different state apparatus, in the form of the Dictatorship of the Proletariat.

This is to stress the fact that the existing state apparatus, which has been set up by the ruling class of capitalists, the bourgeoisie, in order to crush the "lower classes", the proletariat and the family farmers, has to be destroyed. A new state apparatus is required, in order to crush the capitalists, as they make every effort, after the Revolution, to return to power, to"restore their paradise lost".

The alternative, that at the time of the Revolution, the existing state apparatus is *not smashed,* then the current batch of rulers will merely be replaced by different faces, according to Lenin. Nothing of substance will change. The working people will continue to be crushed and exploited.

The only alternative to capitalism is Scientific Socialism, in the form of the Dictatorship of the Proletariat. Lenin makes that quite clear, in State and Revolution.

This book is available for sale, on the internet, and possibly also in audio form. It may even be possible to download it for free. As Venezuela is highly industrialized, it is reasonable to assume that the working class is cultured. No doubt a great many workers have digital devices, or at least have access to such devices.

Bear in mind that in Russia, in the summer of 1917, the Russian common people, workers and family farmers, were far less cultured. Many were illiterate. There was certainly no internet! Yet under far more difficult circumstances, Lenin and the Communist Party were able to raise the level of awareness of the common people, especially the proletariat, to the point that a successful Scientific Socialist revolution could take place. This has gone down in history as the Great October Russian Proletarian Socialist Revolution.

With a supreme effort, on the part of the middle class intellectuals and advanced workers of Venezuela, we can expect to soon see a Great Venezuelan Proletarian Socialist Revolution. I have complete confidence in you!

With Fraternal Communist Greetings,

Gerald McIsaac

CHAPTER 17

BOTH TRUMP AND HARRIS
CHOOSING "RUNNING MATES"

The Republican National Committee, RNC, has now officially endorsed Donald Trump, as their candidate for the office of President, in 2024. Trump, in turn, chose J.D. Vance as his "running mate", the candidate for Vice President. Vance is a Senator from the state of Ohio, considered to be a "swing state".

It is anticipated that on August 19, the Democratic National Committee, DNC, will officially endorse Kamala Harris, as their candidate, for the office of President, in 2024. It is further anticipated that, even before the official endorsement, Harris will choose a suitable "running mate", as the candidate for Vice President. Various officials have been mentioned, with the field narrowed down to three, from the states of Minnesota, Pennsylvania and Arizona. It is not by chance that all three candidates are from states that are considered to be "swing states".

In the stilted political jargon, a "swing state" is "any state that could reasonably be won by either the Democratic or Republican candidate for President".

It stands to reason that the choice of a "running mate", from such a state, makes it far more likely for the candidate for President, to win that state.

Now the mainstream press is conducting a "countdown", the days remaining until the "Presidential Election" of November 5. As well, they are also keeping track of the money being donated to the two "Presidential Campaigns". This money is being measured in "hundreds of millions"!

Each "Campaign" is anticipated to cost *several billion dollars!*

This will culminate on the day voters "go to the polls", of course on November 5, to vote for their candidate for the office of President. Not that American voters get to directly vote for their candidate for the President. Indeed, not. It is not that simple. Under the complicated "electoral system", the candidate, of one of the two Parties, Republican or Democratic, either Trump or Harris, who wins the majority of votes, in a particular state, will in turn receive *all of the Electoral votes, of that state!*

It is reasonable to assume that, shortly after all the votes are counted, probably late in the day of November 5, the bourgeois journalists will be able to announce the next "President Elect of the United States".

The voting of the Electors, who are appointed by the States, as well as the District of Columbia, is a mere "formality", to take place "on or before January 3". Or at least, that is the plan.

There is just one little problem. That which they have planned, all of the aforementioned, is *completely Unconstitutional!* It is in *direct violation* of the *Twelfth Amendment to the Constitution!*

Even though I have reproduced it before, it is of vital importance, so I have chosen to do so again:

Twelfth Amendment

The Electors shall meet in their respective states and vote by ballot for President and Vice-President, one of whom, at least, shall not be an inhabitant of the same state with themselves; they shall name in their ballots the person voted for as President, and in distinct ballots the person voted for as Vice-President, and they shall make distinct lists of all persons voted for as President, and of all persons voted for as Vice-President, and of the number of votes for each, which lists they shall sign and certify, and transmit sealed to the seat of the government of the United States, directed to the President of the Senate;–the President of the Senate shall, in the presence of the Senate and House of Representatives, open all the certificates and the votes shall then be counted;–The person having the greatest number of votes for President, shall be the President, if such number be a majority of the whole number of Electors appointed; and if no person have such majority, then from the persons having the highest numbers not exceeding three on the list of those voted for as President, the House of Representatives shall choose immediately, by ballot, the President. But in choosing the President, the votes shall be taken by states, the representation from each state having one vote; a quorum for this purpose shall consist of a member or members from two-thirds of the states, and a majority of all the states shall be necessary to a choice. [And if the House of Representatives shall not choose a President whenever the right of choice shall devolve upon them, before the fourth day of March next following, then the Vice-President shall act as President, as in case of the death or other constitutional disability of the President.–]The person having the greatest number of votes as Vice-President, shall be the Vice-President, if such number be a majority of the whole number of Electors appointed, and if no person have a majority, then from the two highest numbers on the list, the Senate shall choose the Vice-President; a quorum for the purpose shall consist of two-thirds of the whole number of Senators, and a majority of the whole number shall be necessary to a choice. But no person constitutionally ineligible to the office of President shall be eligible to that of Vice-President of the United States.

By law, *Constitutional law,* there is *no "presidential election"!* There is only a *federal election!* It is the *Electors,* and *only the Electors,* who are appointed by the *States,* and *only by the States,* who get to vote for the individual of *their choice,* for the office of President. As well, those same Electors get to vote, *on a separate ballot,* for the individual of *their choice,* for the office of Vice President. The states have *no right to meddle in a federal election!*

Further, the Twelfth Amendment makes *no mention* of any political party! Nor is there any mention of any "popular vote"! The scheduled November 5 vote is *meaningless!* For that reason, there is *no "President Elect"!* In fact, by *Constitutional Law,* the American voters are *excluded from any federal election!*

As for those who may object that this is hardly democratic, I can only respond *this is the law! Constitutional Law!* Further, all elected federal officials have taken an oath, to *preserve, protect and defend the Constitution!*

Hold those federal officials accountable! Demand that they honor their oath! Demand that the 2024 *federal election* follow the procedure laid out in the Twelfth Amendment! Also demand that both Joe Biden and Kamala Harris be removed from office immediately! Both came to office by means of a fraudulent election!

As for those who may suggest that I am being ridiculous, I can only respond that you are correct. The federal officials are not about to perform their duty! That would never occur to them! The very thought would never cross their minds! Such heresy!

As I have mentioned in various previous articles, my focus is on the "common people", and in particular the working class, the proletariat. That is the class which "holds the future in its hands". It is just not aware of this, or at least, not as yet.

In the interests of raising the level of awareness of the proletariat, it is necessary to expose the monopoly capitalist class, the multi billionaires, the bourgeoisie. That is the class of people in charge. They are running the country. In fact, they are running the country right into the ground! Yet so many working people still believe their lies.

Those same working people pay strict attention to the news, at least as presented by the mainstream press. As well, countless workers are now quite cultured, in possession of various digital devices, so that they have access to the "Leftist" press. All the press is now focused on the "Presidential election", and the two "running mates", for the Presidency. For that reason, we can use this to our advantage.

All "conscious people", those who are aware of the revolutionary theories of Marx and Lenin, must become active. It is your *duty!* The level of awareness of the proletariat must be raised. They, or at least the *most advanced workers*, must become class conscious. The working class, the proletariat, must become aware of themselves as a class, with their own class interests. They must be made aware of those same revolutionary theories. They must be prepared for Scientific Socialism. This can happen only through overthrowing the bourgeoisie, smashing the existing state apparatus, and replacing it with a new state apparatus, in the form of the Dictatorship of the Proletariat.

Middle class attorneys, preferably experts in Constitutional law, must challenge both federal elections, that of 2020 and 2024. Every effort must be made to remove both Biden and Harris from office. As well, the 2024 federal election must follow the procedure laid out in the Twelfth Amendment. These are the arguments which must be made in federal court, preferably the Supreme Court.

Such a court challenge will be closely monitored by the press, both mainstream and Leftist. The working people will be sure to follow all developments, and in the process, receive a valuable education.

There are various other suggestions I have made, in previous articles, concerning the manner in which we can assist the working class, or at least the most advanced members of the proletariat, in becoming true Marxists, Communists. Much as I tire of repeating this, perhaps a brief summary is appropriate.

Flood social media with Leftist literature. Join the two mainstream political parties, as "card carrying members". Take part in marches and demonstrations, as Communists, carrying signs with class content. Unite the various Councils- Soviets- which have spontaneously taken shape. Encourage "celebrities", especially "Hollywood Movie Stars" to become active. Their fans pay strict attention to anything they say!

There is an urgent need for a true Communist Party, one which calls for the Dictatorship of the Proletariat. Middle class intellectuals, in cooperation with the most advanced,"internationalist workers", can take part in that creation.

Encourage all workers to read the Essential Works of Marx and Lenin. The importance of State and Revolution, must be stressed. The Revolution could break out at any moment. It is best to be prepared!

That which the press, rather politely refers to as "popular uprisings", and is in fact revolutionary motion, is taking place in various parts of the world. These include the West European countries of France, Britain and **Germany**, among others.

There are also revolutionary uprisings in South America, in the country of **Venezuela**. In South Asia, the country of Bangladesh is "seething". In West Africa, Nigeria is "in turmoil".

Bear in mind that these "revolutionary motions", these "mass movements", tend to spread, to other countries. It is not just in North America that a Revolution is about to take place!

It was Lenin who foresaw a "World Socialist Republic". Sadly, he was murdered, so that he never lived to see that day. We can only honor his memory by taking his advice, "following in his footsteps", carrying out the policies, that he was able to only outline.

In this way, the younger generation will live to see a world without classes, a world without capitalists fighting to re-divide the world. A world of working people living together in peace. A world of Communism.

That is a goal upon which we can all unite.

Gerald McIsaac

CHAPTER 18

STATEMENT IN SUPPORT OF THE BANGLADESH REVOLUTION

Bangladesh is a densely populated country in South Asia. With a population of 174 million people, it is the eighth most populous country in the world. The country is largely agrarian, with possibly half of the population working in agriculture. Rice is of course the primary staple food crop, as well as wheat and corn, referred to as maize. The cash crops include tea, coffee, cotton, sugarcane, tobacco and jute, otherwise known as burlap.

Yet it also has a considerable amount of industry, especially textile mills, sugar factories, fertilizer factories, cement factories and aluminum works.

These industrial plants are of vital importance, as they employ a great many workers, proletarians. It is these workers who are about to play a key role in the revolution, which Bangladesh is now experiencing.

It is the students who are "spearheading" the revolution. It started when they called for the abolition of the "quota system", in which thirty percent of all government jobs, go to the descendants of the "freedom fighters", those who won the war of independence in 1971.

The Prime Minister, Sheikh Hasina, denied this request, and "cracked down" on the protesters. This involved the use of wide spread violence, on the part of the police and military, which resulted in the death of numerous people. As well, a great many student leaders, and members of opposition parties, were arrested. In addition, a country wide curfew was imposed, along with an internet blackout. The fact that Hasina was referring to these protesters as "traitors and terrorists", did not endear her to them.

These measures did not have the desired effect of "quelling the protests". On the contrary, the protests "spiraled into a campaign of social disobedience, all across the nation, worsening by the day, with more and more people joining the students", according to the journalists.

In fact, the student led protests spread all across the country, so that all "common people", workers and farmers, from all walks of life, young and old, joined the students in demanding the end to the quota system.

This placed a great deal of pressure on the government, so that the quota system was annulled. Perhaps it was thought that this would satisfy the protesters, as their demands were being met. It most certainly did not. Instead, their demands merely changed, increased to that of demanding the resignation of the Prime Minister, Sheikh Hasina.

To those of us who are "conscious people", which is to say Marxists, Communists, this came as no great surprise. After all, according to Marx, "Reforms are a byproduct of revolutionary motion. They merely serve to strengthen and further the revolutionary movement".

It is estimated that in the capital city of Dhaka alone, a "crowd" of possibly four hundred thousand people defied the curfew, and marched on the "most highly guarded residence in the country", the private home of the Prime Minister, Sheikh Hasina.

The journalists report that the "mob" ignored the police, military and armored vehicles, and "stormed the home of Prime Minister Hasina". Those who were guarding that building, rather wisely decided to "step aside".

In a state of shock and disbelief, with mere minutes to spare, Hasina was able to jump on a helicopter and escape to India. Rather than facing the people she has been "leading", for the last fifteen years, she chose to seek political asylum, in a foreign country.

Even though she was allowed to enter India, it is not clear that she is entirely welcome. The "Indian Intelligence Services" have placed Hasina in "protective custody", and moved her to an "undisclosed location". She has been granted permission for an "interim stay". (Bear in mind that interim means temporary)

Other countries also, are "less than enthusiastic" about accepting her. The United States has rescinded her passport, and the United Kingdom has reportedly "shut its doors", at least temporarily.

By contrast, Bangladesh is certainly anxious to welcome her back! They have even requested that India arrest Hasina, and send her back, so that she can face criminal charges.

As a result of this revolution, the curfew has been lifted, and all previously arrested "protesters" have been released from jail. They even succeeded in dissolving Parliament.

Into this "power vacuum", an "interim government" is being created, with Mohamed Yunus as the "chief advisor". He is a very popular figure, an "entrepreneur, banker and economist", the winner of a Nobel Peace Prize, for "pioneering the concepts of micro credit and micro finance".

It is perhaps not too surprising that the army has plans of their own. The Army Chief of Staff is calling for people to have "faith and trust" in the army, as the army promises to "protect the lives and property of people", to "bring peace and harmony back to the country", to "stop the violence, murders, looting, hooliganism and protests".

In other words, the Army Chief of Staff wants to *crush the revolution!*

These plans include taking over the interim government. As the Army Chief of Staff stated, "Now we will form an interim government and continue our work to lead the country. The country is witnessing a period of revolution right now. I have invited all the leaders of the political parties. They came here and we had a good discussion. We have decided to form an interim government. Through the interim government, all the functioning of the government will take place."

From this, it is clear that the army and all "opposition parties", plans to replace the rule of Hasina and her political party, with their own rule!

The leaders of the revolution have made it perfectly clear, that they are opposed to the plan of the army, to seize power! As they stated, "We do not want a military government, this is not just the end of the tyrant Hasina, we are going to ensure a citizen's government…. We were ignored by authorities when we were protesting peacefully to reform the quota system. They thought that the students would get tired after protesting for two days. But because they were mistaken, it is no longer a quota reform protest. It's been turned into a protest to reform the state. The state must take responsibility for all those who have been killed and injured so far…. what we need is a citizen's charter, we need a civilian government, and we are going to ensure it".

It is clear that the Bangladesh revolution is far from over! Now that Hasina has been removed from office, the common people have now secured some democratic rights, and not just on paper.

We can compare this to the revolutionary situation which existed in Russia, immediately after the Emperor, Czar Nicholas was overthrown, in February of 1917.

At that time, the capitalists seized power, and established a democratic republic. This provided the common people, workers and family farmers, referred to as peasants, with some democratic rights, if only on paper. Yet it did not provide them with much more.

They remained largely poverty stricken, hungry and cold, still at war with Germany and the Central Powers, longing for "peace, land and bread". Their new government responded with an abundance of promises. Nothing else. Sound familiar?

Yet Lenin, who was in exile, was able to return to Russia, in April of that year. He found that, as a result of the revolution, there existed a "dual power" in Russia. On the one hand, there was the state power of the capitalists, as was expressed in the government, and supported those capitalists. On the other hand, there was the "Soviet Power", in that Soviet Means Council, which represented the common people, the workers, military personnel and farmers.

The "state power", of the Soviets, was almost as strong as that of the capitalists! For that reason, the capitalists dared not arrest Lenin, as soon as he stepped off the train, much as they desired to do so.

The fact is that revolutionary motion frequently gives rise to Soviets. It is a spontaneous creation of working people. They first appeared in Russia, in the first revolution of 1905. They reappeared in 1917. They have since appeared in numerous other revolutions. It is entirely possible that they have also been created in Bangladesh.

Assuming that is the case, then those Soviets are the nucleus of a new state power. These may take the shape of Soviets of Workers, Farmers, Military and possibly Intellectuals. It is these Soviets which are destined to assume power in Bangladesh.

As yet, the leaders of the Bangladesh revolution are not speaking in class terms. They are speaking merely in terms of democracy, and that is certainly a step in the right direction. Now they have to be made aware that democracy is nothing other than a method of *class rule!* It is a form of government in which one *class,* in this case the *ruling class* of *capitalists,* subjugates all *lower classes!* The classes of workers and farmers. For that reason, no democratic republic can be inclusive! The government can represent *only the class in power!*

In this case, the ruling class is that of the capitalists, technically referred to as the bourgeoisie. The "lower classes" include the family farmers, also known as peasants, and the working class, technically referred to as proletarians.

This brings us to that which the protesters refer to as a "civilian government". This is really a "state apparatus", or a "state machine", to put it in popular terms. Such an apparatus has been set up, by the ruling class of capitalists, in order to *crush* the "lower classes", the workers and family farmers. This apparatus includes that of the police, military, courts, prisons and other "coercive institutions".

It is not at all surprising that the Army Chief of Staff wants to *quell* the revolution, to *restore "peace and harmony"*. As part of the state apparatus, one which supports the ruling class of capitalists, the leaders of the Army are most emphatically *counter revolutionary!*

Incidentally, by contrast, the "rank and file" members of the military, the "enlisted personnel", and not just those of the army, also tend to be revolutionary. Not too surprising, as most of them are workers and farmers.

Now to return to the fact that the leaders of the army want to seize power, to "form an interim government".

Their plan is to *seize control* of the existing state apparatus, which was abandoned by Hasina, as she fled the country.

It should be noted that this "state apparatus" is *treasured*, by the capitalists! Even the Crown Jewels could not be more highly valued! Or protected!

Now with Hasina "out of the way", this has created that which is referred to as a "power vacuum". She may be gone, but she left behind the "state apparatus"! It is still very much intact! Just waiting for someone to gain possession!

It is this supremely valuable state apparatus which is now "up for grabs"! The leaders of various political parties, as well as the leaders of the army, are determined to seize control of that apparatus, and set themselves up, as the new rulers!

This is to stress the fact that the existing state apparatus, which has been established by the capitalists, with the sole purpose of *crushing* the working people, *cannot* be used for *any other purpose!* It must be *destroyed! Smashed!*

It is up to the revolutionaries to *smash* the existing state apparatus, as it cannot be used to crush the capitalists, *after* the revolution. Yet their resistance will "increase tenfold", after they lose power, as they make every effort to "restore their paradise lost", according to Lenin.

For that reason, a *new* state apparatus is required, to be established *after* the revolution. This apparatus is known as the *Dictatorship of the Proletariat!* Lenin explains this supremely well in his master piece, State and Revolution.

To put this book in historical perspective, it was written in the summer of 1917, in preparation for the Russian Great October Socialist Proletarian Revolution, of that same year. That revolution was successful, because it followed the advice of Lenin.

Now it is up to the leaders of the Bangladesh revolution to become *class conscious,* to *raise their level of awareness*, to become *aware* of the revolutionary theories of Marx and Lenin.

They can then bring that revolutionary awareness to the "common people", the workers and family farmers, or at least to the most advanced strata of those classes. Those advanced members will in turn explain it to the less advanced.

In this way, the Bangladesh revolutionaries will secure their "citizens government", one which will "hold accountable", those responsible for the death of so many innocent people. There is no other way! The existing state apparatus cannot be *reformed!*

Although this is indeed a "tall order", it is nowhere near as difficult as it once was. A careful reading of the essential works of Marx and Lenin will be sufficient, at least for the present. At a bare minimum, State and Revolution, by Lenin, is absolutely required. That work is readily available on the internet.

A proper understanding of that work will "pave the way" towards a successful Bangladesh Great Proletarian Socialist Revolution.

With Fraternal Revolutionary Communist Greetings,

Gerald McIsaac

CHAPTER 19

DEMOCRATIC NATIONAL CONVENTION, 2024

Now that President Joe Biden has "dropped out of the race", as he "decided not to run for re-election", he has decided to "pass the torch" to his Vice President, Kamala Harris. Now it is up to Harris, to make the Democratic Party proud, to bless the country with its first female President, and a "Black Female President", at that. Or at least, so say the political pundits.

In fact, Biden was forced to step aside. The ruling class of monopoly capitalists, the multi billionaires, the bourgeoisie, decided that he had to go, for whatever reason. The fact that Biden is very feeble, and probably suffering from dementia, was very likely a factor in this decision. As well, Trump was trouncing Biden in the polls. Better to "place someone else" in the White House, someone more "reasonable" than Trump, someone who can be counted upon to do as they are told. That "certain someone", that more "reasonable" person, is Kamala Harris.

The appointment of Kamala Harris, as the nominee of the Democratic Party, by the Democratic National Convention, is a mere formality. There is no harm in this. The harm comes when the American voters are forced to choose between the two candidates, of the two mainstream political parties, Democratic and Republican, for the office of the Presidency. Especially as they have nothing to say about this!

In fact, it is completely illegal. Unconstitutional. A violation of the Twelfth Amendment to the Constitution. As I have published that Amendment in previous articles, along with the fact that the whole "November Presidential Election" process is completely illegal, there is no need to repeat it here.

Of course, the mainstream press is well aware of this, but makes no mention of this "little detail", this perversion of the federal election. Completely understandable, as that same press serves the class of people in charge, the monopoly capitalists, the multi billionaires, the bourgeoisie. Yet the "Leftist" press, the "Underground" press, is also remaining silent! Strange but true. And completely unacceptable!

These "November Presidential Elections" give rise to fraudulent Presidents, and fraudulent Vice Presidents. Just as Biden is a fraudulent President, so too, Harris is a fraudulent Vice President. And now she is determined to become a fraudulent President!

At the moment, the press is reporting that a great many protesters have flocked to Chicago, "Ahead of the DNC". If nothing else, they are very loud and clear, "making their voices heard". The journalists report that they are "calling attention to abortion rights, economic injustice and the war in Gaza". They also maintain that their "mission remains the same", that they "learned their lesson from the RNC", that they "predict bigger crowds and more robust demonstrations".

If only that were true! If only they had "learned their lesson"! They have not learned a thing! They are merely repeating the same mistakes! Only louder!

These "bigger crowds and more robust demonstrations", merely amount to an increase in volume. People are already well aware of the fact, that the American government supports the Israeli's, in their "War In Gaza". Yet protesters are screaming this, at the top of their lungs!

The fact is that the American government represents the interests of the ruling class of monopoly capitalists, the bourgeoisie. Those same capitalists have decided to support the government of Israel, no matter what. President Biden merely does as he is told. Assuming Vice President Harris becomes President, as is very likely, she too, will do as she is told. Different faces, serving the same class.

No amount of "bellowing", on the part of the protesters, will change that fact.

What is needed is not more noise, but an increase- a dramatic increase! - in the *level of awareness* of the working class, the proletariat. It has to become *class conscious*, aware of the existence of classes, and the irreconcilable differences between those classes.

The conditions of life, of the working class, does not lead to the awareness of itself, as a class. Nor are they aware of the fact that they are in a constant state of war with the monopoly capitalist class, the bourgeoisie. This war is usually quiet, hidden below the surface, but it occasionally flares up, into open rebellion. Revolution. We are close to a full blown Revolution.

As Marx stated, in the Communist Manifesto:

"The history of all hitherto existing society is the history of class struggles.

"Freeman and slave, patrician and plebeian, lord and serf, guild-master and journeyman, in a word, oppressor and oppressed, stood in constant opposition to one another, carried on an uninterrupted, now hidden, now open fight, a fight that each time ended, either in a revolutionary reconstitution of society at large, or in the common ruin of the contending classes".

Now we are at the point that the "class struggle", of the "oppressor and oppressed", of the proletariat with the bourgeoisie, is about to become an "open fight", which is about to end in a "reconstitution of society at large". This "open fight" is referred to as a Revolution, and the resulting "reconstitution of society at large", is referred to as Scientific Socialism, in the form of the Dictatorship of the Proletariat.

As yet, the working class, the proletariat, is not aware of this. It is the duty of conscious people, those who are aware of the revolutionary theories of Marx and Lenin, to bring that awareness to the working class. The most advanced workers must be raised to the level of conscious people, referred to as Communists.

Lenin explains this supremely well, in his excellent work, What Is To Be Done? As he stated, in reference to the history of the Russian proletariat, "the workers were not, and could not, be conscious of the irreconcilable antagonisms of their interests to the whole of the modern political and social system.... This consciousness could only be brought to them from without. The history of all countries show that the working class, exclusively by its own efforts, is able to develop only trade union consciousness, that is, it may itself realize the necessity for combining in unions, for fighting against the employers and for striving to compel the government to pass necessary labor legislation, etc. The theory of socialism, however, grew out of the philosophic, historical and economic theories that were elaborated by the educated representatives of the propertied classes, the intellectuals. According to their social status, the founders of modern scientific socialism, Marx and Engels, themselves belonged to the bourgeois intelligentsia."

We can add that Lenin also, was a middle class intellectual, an attorney by training. I mention this for the benefit of certain working class people, those who are prejudiced against middle class intellectuals. *Get over it!* Such a prejudice can only work in favor of the capitalists, and do great harm to the revolutionary motion.

It is our duty, that of conscious people, previously referred to as Social Democrats, or Bolsheviks, now referred to as Communists, to bring this awareness to the working class, to explain to them the revolutionary Scientific Socialist theories of Marx and Lenin.

This class struggle can be compared to a boxing match, in which one of the boxers is blindfolded, swinging wildly in all directions. No doubt, an occasional blow will be landed, but strictly by chance. Of course, the other boxer, being able to see quite well, is able to land blow after blow.

In this extremely over simplified comparison, the boxer who is blindfolded, is of course the working class, the proletariat. The boxer who can see very well is the monopoly capitalist class, the bourgeoisie. Rest assured, the capitalists are supremely class conscious!

The "solution" to the problem, is quite simple: Remove the blindfold. In class terms, this means raising the level of awareness of the proletariat, so that they are class conscious, aware of themselves as a class, with their own class interests. In this way, they can focus on striking out against their class enemies, the monopoly capitalists, as opposed to swinging wildly.

Of necessity, class consciousness includes becoming aware of the revolutionary theories of Marx and Lenin. The working class, or at least the most advanced workers, must become familiar with those theories. Those advanced workers will in turn, lead the less advanced.

Now to return to the protests at the DNC.

Of all the signs and posters that were displayed on the internet, only one made any reference to class content. That was a poster by the Green Party of the United States, GPSU, which stated, "We Need A New Party For The Working People".

That is most emphatically true! We need a new Party, but not that of the Green Party. They have a Party Platform of "nonviolence, social justice, environmentalism, grassroots democracy, anti-war, anti-racism". Pacifist nonsense!

We need a true Communist Party, one which calls for the Dictatorship of the Proletariat. Scientific Socialism! That is the one and only alternative to monopoly capitalism!

It is only such a Communist Party which can properly lead the working class, can raise the level of awareness of the proletariat, in preparation for the Dictatorship of the Proletariat.

Working people need to hear about the revolutionary theories of Marx and Lenin! They need to become class conscious! At least the most advanced workers must be raised to the level of true Communists!

In the absence of a true Communist Party, one which calls for the Dictatorship of the Proletariat, we can still raise the consciousness of the proletariat, if only by becoming involved in the struggles which interest them, and in the process, explaining the class conflict.

At the moment, working people are focused on the DNC, and the protesters. For that reason, we need to make sure that the protesters carry signs and posters, which contain class content.

It is best if these posters are written in a manner which is entertaining. After all, the best way to educate people, is by entertaining them, at the same time. Such details are best left to entertainment specialists. Or as working people phrase it, "never tell a mechanic how to pull a wrench"!

Having said that, it is important that workers be made aware of the fact that the scientific name for their class, is that of proletariat. They must also be made aware that the scientific name of the monopoly capitalist class, is that of bourgeoisie. The current lack of awareness, of the proletariat, of the scientifically correct class terms, is used by the capitalists, against the working class.

As well, such posters must call for Revolution, for the over throw of the bourgeoisie, for Scientific Socialism, in the form of the Dictatorship of the Proletariat. We will know that we are being successful, that the level of awareness of the working class is being raised, when these expressions become common place.

This brings us to the "legal front", so to speak, one which is closely followed by the workers.

With that in mind, may I suggest a court challenge to the "November Presidential Election", as it is in direct violation of the Twelfth Amendment. Unconstitutional.

No doubt, there are people who may object that the Twelfth Amendment is hardly democratic, as it does not allow the voters to cast a ballot for their President and Vice President. True. But that is not the issue. The fact is that the democratic republic must be defended. Every effort must be made, to force the government to abide by the Constitution. That is a matter of principle.

It is of the utmost importance to defend our democratic rights, as they are constantly under attack, by the capitalists. These democratic rights include that of a free and fair "federal election", as guaranteed in the Constitution. There is no mention of a "November Presidential Election", in the Constitution! Nor is there any mention of any political party! The voters have *nothing to say,* concerning any federal election! As well, the states have *no right to meddle* in any federal election! Forcing the Electors to vote for a particular candidate, of one political party, is *Unconstitutional!*

It is up to the Electors to choose an individual *of their choice,* for the office of President, as well as an individual *of their choice,* for the office of Vice President. *As per the Constitution!*

We will know that the protesters have indeed "learned their lesson", when those same protesters challenge the "November Presidential Election" in a court of law. We can only "dream of the day", when middle class attorneys, experts on Constitutional law, stand before the Supreme Court, making these arguments.

Without doubt, the working people will be closely following these proceedings. For that reason, it is up to conscious people, Communists, to explain to those people, in terms they can understand, that which is happening. This, in turn, will serve to raise the level of awareness of the proletariat.

To have the Supreme Court declare the "November Presidential Election" to be Unconstitutional, is to be regarded as a bonus. It is also quite likely. At that point, the Electors will be allowed to vote for the individual of their choice, for the office of President, and on a separate ballot, vote for the individual of their choice, for the office of Vice President.

The "individual" they vote for as President, could well be Kamala Harris. Or not. As well, the "individual" they vote for as Vice President, could well be her "running mate". Or not. That is entirely at the discretion of the Electors. As per Constitutional law.

For the moment, may the signs and posters also read:

Workers of the World, Unite!
Scientific Socialism!
Dictatorship of the Proletariat!

CHAPTER 20

STRIKE AT BOTH CANADIAN RAILROADS

Canada has two main railroads, Canadian National Railroad, and Canadian Pacific Kansas City Railroad, commonly referred to as CN Rail, and CP Rail. On August 22, 2024, for the first time in history, both Railroads went on strike, at the same time.

Even before the anticipated strike date, the Railroads refused to transport certain articles, perishable goods, such as meat and medicines, as well as hazardous materials, including chlorine.

This strike, or "labour dispute", to use the stilted jargon of the capitalists, is expected to have a "ripple effect" across the country, and beyond. One immediate effect, within the country, is that a great many commuters, in several large cities, will have to secure a different means of transportation.

Without doubt, the bourgeois economists are correct, when they say that "Canada relies on rail". After all, perhaps one billion dollars' worth of goods are transported, each day, across the country. With the Railroads shut down, we can expect "supply chain hold ups", so that "both small and large businesses", will be "effected".

The fact is that all businesses, large and small, make a supreme effort to "reduce their inventory", to keep as little "capital on hand", as possible. Rather than "stock up", in preparation "for a rainy day", as working people do, they are careful to keep as little as possible, on hand.

In this way, they are able to keep taxes to a minimum. After all, the more stock they have on hand, the more taxes they are forced to pay.

The two Railways are represented by the same Teamsters Union, but for reasons which defy rational explanation, negotiate separate contracts. Up until the present, the contracts have been careful to expire at different times, so that never before, have both Railroads been on strike, simultaneously. In this way, a strike by one Railroad allowed the other Railroad to "take up the slack", thus reducing the pressure on the capitalists, to negotiate a fair settlement.

According to the internet, "A one-year contract extension at CN Rail, in 2022, led to its contracts lining up with CPKC Rail, which expired in 2023. The Teamsters Canada Rail Conference has been in negotiations since then".

Clearly the workers have been working without a contract, since the start of the year. The fact that the Teamsters Union was able to force negotiations to take place, with both companies, at the same time, increases their leverage.

It is significant that this strike is completely legal, as according to a decision of the Supreme Court of Canada, on January 30, 2015, "the right to strike is Constitutionally protected", at least for workers who are not classified as providing "essential services". The Railroad workers are not classified as an essential service.

Both Railroad companies responded to these strikes, by imposing a "lock out". This is a tactic the companies use, that of preventing the workers from entering the workplace to work, during a strike, which is precisely the very thing the workers are refusing to do. Even though this makes no sense, it is meant to pressure the workers to accept a new contract.

On the first day of the strike, on August 22, the leader of the New Democratic Party, Jagmeet Singh, visited the workers on strike in Montreal, and expressed his support for them. He told the workers that if necessary, he will vote against back to work legislation.

The ruling Liberal Party, led by Justin Trudeau, was clearly in favour of a "negotiated settlement", between the Railroads and the Teamsters Union. That was made abundantly clear, up until the day of the Railroad strike. On that day, the government made it quite clear that the strike was not acceptable. The very height of hypocrisy!

With a view to ending this "labour dispute", the Labour Minister "passed the buck" to the Canada Industrial Relations Labour Board, CIRLB.

In an attempt to "do an end run", around the Supreme Court ruling, which guarantees the workers the Constitutional "right to strike", the Labour Board applied a rather obscure rule, of the Canada Labour Code:

"Under section 107 of the Canada Labour Code, the Minister of Labour can refer the dispute to the Canada Industrial Relations Board (CIRB) for binding arbitration and prohibit a strike, lockout or end any ongoing stoppage pending a resolution. Alternatively, the government can also reconvene Parliament and introduce back-to-work legislation".

As the Parliament was not sitting, it was up to the CIRB to "take action". They immediately ruled that the strike by CN Rail was illegal, *despite the Supreme Court ruling,* and ordered them back to work.

The response of the Teamsters Union was to return to work, at CN Rail, but at the same time to issue CN Rail with a 72-hour strike notice, so that they will be in a legal position to strike by August 25. CPKC Rail was already in a legal position to strike, so they were not forced back to work.

Then, according to the press, on Aug 24, the government issued a surprise ruling:

"The Federal Labour Board Orders Rail employees back to work, on Saturday, after three days. Work to start Monday, to continue until binding arbitration process is complete. Also ruled that the contract between CN and the Union, that expired on December 31, has now been extended, until a new agreement comes into effect".

In response to this ruling, a Spokesman for the Teamsters **Union** had this to say:

"The two major railways in Canada manufactured this crisis, took the country hostage, and manipulated the country once again, disregarding the rights afforded to working class Canadians. The government took this unprecedented step, using this seldom utilized section of the labour code, only because they knew their minority could not gather the support needed to pass a legislated resolution to appease the railroads".

This reference to a "minority", requires an explanation.

The Prime Minister of Canada, has to be a member of the Party which has the majority of seats, within Parliament. As no one Party currently has a majority, it was necessary to form a "coalition government", of two Parties. Those two Parties are the Liberal Party and New Democratic Party. Taken together, the two Parties have a majority in Parliament.

The Teamsters Union is correct when they state that the "minority", the Liberal Party, "could not gather the support needed to pass a legislated resolution". The NDP would merely oppose it!

In fact, such an attempt, by the Liberal government, to legislate the Railroad workers back to work, would almost certainly fail, and probably lead to a "no confidence vote", which would force a federal election. That is the last thing the Liberals want!

The President of the Teamsters Canada Rail Conference, stated his response in somewhat stronger terms:

"This decision by the CIRB sets a dangerous precedent. It signals to corporate Canada that large companies need only stop their operations for a few hours, inflict short term economic pain, and the federal government will step in to break a Union. The rights of Canadian workers have been significantly diminished today".

It is significant that these statements make references to the existence of classes, and to the fact that the government represents the interests of the ruling class of capitalists. The first statement even mentions the working class, while the second statement refers to "large companies" and "corporate Canada". This is a none too subtle reference to the multi billionaires, the monopoly capitalists, the bourgeoisie, the class of people who rule the country.

It is to the credit of the Teamsters Union, that they plan to fight this ruling, in federal court. As the President of Teamsters Canada stated, "our legal team is looking at all our options now". They are determined to defend the Constitutional right of all Canadians, to engage in strike action. Bravo, Teamsters Union!

The Director of CN Rail has issued a statement, which can **only** be considered to be an attack upon the working class. He says the jobs provided, by the Railroad, "are not minimum wage", that "they pay one hundred twenty thousand for a conductor, and one hundred fifty thousand for a locomotive engineer".

That may well be true, but is *no* reason to not fight for higher wages. After all, wages are "tied together". It may help to think of this as "invisible chains", linking the wages of all workers. If the wages of the highest paid workers go up, so too, the wages of the lowest paid workers go up. It follows that the way to raise the wages of the lowest paid workers, is to raise the wages of the highest paid workers. For that reason, workers should always fight for higher wages. We all benefit!

Allow me to stress the fact, that this is true, only under capitalism. Under Scientific Socialism, a far different social system, we will have a far different economic system, so that we can focus on directly raising the wages of the lowest paid workers.

As I write this, it is Sunday, August 25, and the workers have been ordered to go back to work on Monday morning.

It has been reported that a "case management meeting" will be held on Thursday, August 29, with the "Board and Parties involved", to discuss the "binding arbitration process".

Without doubt, the striking Railroad workers are angry and frustrated. They have the strong Teamsters Union fighting for them, using every legally available option, but that is not enough. They also need to become *class conscious,* aware of the existence of classes, the war between the classes, of the necessity of revolution, and the subsequent Dictatorship of the Proletariat. Scientific Socialism.

These Railroad workers are in the vanguard of the Canadian working class revolutionary motion. They deserve our complete support. Perhaps the best support can come in the form of copies of State and Revolution, and Left Wing Communism, An Infantile Disorder, by Lenin. Of course, there is also the "Essential Works of Lenin", which include What Is To Be Done? as well as Imperialism, the Highest Stage of Capitalism. The Communist Manifesto, by Marx and Engels, is a basic work.

In this way, they will become aware that their struggle, for better wages and working conditions, is part of the broader struggle, of the working class, against the class of **monopoly** capitalists, the multi billionaires, the bourgeoisie. Until they are overthrown, and crushed, under the Dictatorship of the Proletariat, nothing of substance will change.

We will know that we are being successful, when the posters, carried by striking workers, read something more than "on strike". They will also contain revolutionary slogans, such as:

Workers of the World, Unite!
Scientific Socialism!
Dictatorship of the Proletariat!

CHAPTER 21

FIRST PRESIDENTIAL DEBATE: DISASTER FOR TRUMP!

On Tuesday, September 10, the "First Presidential Debate of 2024", between "Former President Donald Trump", and "Vice President Kamala Harris", took place. All of the mainstream news outlets covered this event, broadcasting live, during "prime time", as they knew that countless people were about to watch this performance. Those viewers were hoping to be entertained, and they were not disappointed.

It is clear that the "handlers" of Harris, her coaches, earned they pay! They deserve a raise! She marched onto that stage, as if she owned it, approached Trump with her hand extended, which took him by surprise, and shook his hand. She said, "I am Kamala Harris". In this way, she **took** control, placed Trump on the defensive, and maintained control throughout the "Debate". Bravo, Kamala Harris!

After the "Debate", the journalists were unanimous in their opinion that Harris was "well coached", that she "prosecuted this debate with surgical precision", that her "previous experience as a prosecutor", was put to good use. She looked directly into the camera, when speaking. Her "body language", facial expressions and gestures, were "flawless". When not speaking, she looked closely at Trump.

By contrast, Trump kept looking down, clearly on the defensive. The contrast was striking! As Harris continued to "bait" him, Trump resorted to anger. Perhaps one of his most outrageous accusations, was that of suggesting that Harris was a Marxist! Comrade Kamala! She most certainly is not a Marxist!

Among the lies Trump spoke, perhaps the most ridiculous is that, within the city of Springfield, "immigrants are eating the cats and dogs of the residents". If nothing else, this got a good laugh, from the viewers.

The response of the mainstream media was typical, at least for the most part. They are focused on the effect this may have on the "undecided voters", especially in the "swing states", as they are concerned with the Electoral College. More on that subject, later on in this article.

The exception was that of a certain bourgeois journalist, who provided the gentlest possible criticism of the "richest people in Manhattan". He maintains that the **members** of the Economic Club of New York, invited Donald Trump to speak. The journalist took exception to that. I have chosen to reproduce it, as best I can, as he actually made a few significant statements, which deserve our attention:

"All the rich people I know are smart, but there are a lot of stupid rich people. New Yorks' stupidest rich people gathered in a room and proved how stupid they are. …The Economic Club of New York met in Manhattan…. All are safe and live and work in New York City…. The members of that Club are not economists, mostly Wall Street types, who do not have a graduate degree in anything, never produced anything, have spent their lives massaging money.

"Every one of them has gotten much, much richer, during the four years of the Biden - Harris administration. Now I knew how stupid the speaker was, (Donald Trump- GM) before he opened his mouth. But I did not know how stupid so many members of the New York Economic Club were, until I heard the reactions to the stupidest person who has ever spoken to them. Trump said that RFK Jr. had endorsed him. Trump fired dozens of former officials, who now oppose his election. In answer to a question about child care, his answer, 'child care is child care'.

"The stupidest rich people in New York, gave a huge round of applause. The applause to that huge jumble of words is most disturbing, but then Trump promised all of them another huge tax cut. Those stupid rich people, clapping for the man who tried to overthrow the results of the presidential election, clapping for a man who says 'child care is child care', or clapping because he promised all of them another huge tax cut. Those stupid rich people are willing to corrupt American democracy for the stupidest person who has ever spoken to them. They proved who they really are. The question to 'make child care affordable'. The guy talking is not the problem. It is those people clapping, that has brought this country to this crisis point, in its history as a democracy".

The preceding was not copied in precisely the manner in which it was spoken, because the wording was too non sensical. His speech was disjointed, apologetic and **contradictory**, but for all its faults, a criticism of the "rich people".

This bourgeois journalist was making a supreme effort to not offend the "rich people", to use his words. Of course he was referring to the multi billionaires, the monopoly capitalists, the members of the class of people who are technically referred to as the bourgeoisie. In so doing, he ended up sounding completely ridiculous. Yet strangely, certain parts of what he said were correct. As this is most unusual, coming from a bourgeois journalist, it merits closer examination.

He is correct when he states that "the members of the Economic Club of New York…. live and work in New York City ….in complete safety". True! They are "completely safe" because they can afford to hire bodyguards!

He is also correct when he states that the "members of that Club …. never produced anything, have spent their lives massaging money". Once again, true! The members of the class of monopoly capitalists, the bourgeoisie, produce nothing! They are parasites! Leaches on society! Blood suckers!

It is also a fact that those multi billionaires have become "much, much richer, during the four years of the Biden- Harris administration".

The fact is that the Democratic Party is every bit the loyal and devoted servant of the bourgeoisie, as is the Republican Party! They serve the same class! The Democratic Party is not the "Party of the little guy", the "common people", the working class!

Now for a "reality check"! The members of the class of bourgeoisie, the multi billionaires, the "rich people"- as he refers to them- are not entirely stupid! Bear in mind the old adage, "A fool and his money are soon separated!" And rest assured, countless people, especially other multi billionaires, are only too anxious to separate their "brethren", fellow multi billionaires, from their hard stolen wealth!

Yet those same "rich people", multi billionaires, have found certain liars and fools to be quite useful. That includes Donald Trump.

The journalist was very upset that the audience applauded, after Trump said "child care is child care". Yet that is not the reason they applauded! They applauded because Trump promised them "another huge tax cut".

The journalist is also correct, when he pointed out that the multi billionaires "are willing to corrupt American democracy", although not for the sake of Trump, but for the sake of profit, of not paying taxes. He is also correct when he states that Trump is "not the problem". The "problem" is the "people clapping", the multi billionaires, the bourgeoisie, the class of people who have "brought this country to this crisis point, in its history as a democracy".

The mere fact that a bourgeois journalist was able to point out the lies and hypocrisy of the monopoly capitalists, the bourgeoisie, if only in a most disjointed, apologetic manner, is significant. It is an indication of the strength of the revolutionary motion.

Even though the presentation was halting and barely comprehensible, without any direct reference to the bourgeoisie, it was still a criticism of that class, and could well result in his dismissal.

It is reasonable to expect something better from the independent, Leftist journalists, those who do not work for the mainstream press. After all, they do not have to face the constant threat of being fired.

This is precisely what we find in a report by Ring of Fire, a Leftist broadcast. In reference to that same "Trump - Harris Debate", this journalist pointed out that the Electoral College is "idiotic", that it "disenfranchises millions of people".

The Electoral College is anything but "idiotic". It is the *law. Constitutional law!* The fact that it "disenfranchises millions of people", is the whole idea! That is the *purpose* of the Electoral College!

More accurately, the Electoral College disenfranchises *all American voters,* not "just" millions of people! The popular vote is a *fraud! Unconstitutional!*

As I have documented in previous articles, the Electoral College is a remnant of slavery. It was set up to allow a slave owner to become President.

The Twelfth Amendment to the Constitution documents the procedure to be followed, in all *federal elections!* It is the *Electors,* and *only the Electors,* who are appointed by the *States,* and *only the States,* who have the authority to vote for the candidate, *of their choice,* for the office of President, as well as the candidate, *of their choice,* for the office of Vice President.

This procedure was not followed in the 2020 Presidential Election. For that reason, Biden is a fraudulent President, and Harris is a fraudulent Vice President.

Remarkably enough, Trump is correct, when he states that the 2020 Presidential election was fraudulent. Not for the reasons he gives, but because it did not follow the procedure laid out in the Constitution.

With that in mind, may I suggest to my fellow Leftist journalists, that we all demand that our democratically elected politicians, those who have taken an oath, to "preserve, protect and defend the Constitution", do just that. Their duty!

Granted, that is not about to happen. Yet in the process of making these demands, the level of awareness of the working class, the proletariat, will be raised. They will become more class conscious.

Further, in the interests of giving those misguided souls a little nudge, in the right direction, may I suggest a court challenge. Preferably the Supreme Court could be asked to rule on the legality of the 2020 "Presidential" Election. Not to mention the forthcoming 2024 *Federal Election!*

Bear in mind that the "Trump- Harris Debate" was aired in prime time! Because countless working people watched that spectacle! They are focused on the "Presidential Election"! We can use this to our advantage, to raise the level of awareness of the working class!

Those same working people can be expected to pay strict attention, to any such court challenge. No doubt, they will be surprised, and disappointed, to learn that they have no legal right to vote, in any federal election. We can expect them to demand change! That is the last thing the monopoly capitalists want!

This can be thought of as preparation for revolution, and the subsequent Scientific Socialism, in the form of the Dictatorship of the Proletariat.

I am supremely well aware of the fact that most of my Leftist journalist colleagues, if not all of them, are not Marxists. Most of them think that Socialism may be a good idea, but simply not possible. Sadly, they believe that which is taught in University. The Scientific Socialist theories of Marx and Lenin are not so much taught in University, as distorted.

These independent Leftist journalists are, for the most part, honest, law abiding, tax paying citizens, determined to "make a difference", to "change the system from within", to "enact reforms". They deserve the whole hearted support, from those of us who are Marxists.

Without doubt, they will learn, from their own bitter experience, as well as from the revolutionary motion, that the monopoly capitalists, the "super rich", the multi billionaires, the bourgeoisie, are *in power,* and fully intend to remain *in power!*

With that in mind, may I suggest, to my fellow Leftist journalists, that they once again read the revolutionary works of Marx and Lenin, this time with an open mind.

Bear in mind that capitalism did not always exist. It came into existence with the industrial revolution, as did the creation of two new *revolutionary* classes, the bourgeoisie and the proletariat.

I deliberately emphasized the word *revolutionary,* as the working class, the proletariat, is still revolutionary. This stands in stark contrast to the bourgeoisie, which is now completely reactionary, counter revolutionary.

Now it is up to the working class, the revolutionary proletariat, to overthrow the completely reactionary capitalist class, the bourgeoisie.

There is a sense of urgency to this, to put it politely. Bear in mind that all previous civilizations have risen to a peak, and then fell into decline. Our civilization has also past its peak, and is in decline. Yet our civilization is the one and only civilization to have experienced an industrial revolution.

It is the *revolutionary proletariat* which is *destined* to *reverse the decline* of our civilization. That is a *fundamental tenet of Marxism!* That can only be accomplished by *overthrowing* the bourgeoisie, and establishing a state of *Scientific Socialism,* in the form of the *Dictatorship of the Proletariat!*

As yet, the proletariat is not aware of this, because the conditions of life, of the working class, do not lead to the awareness of itself, as a class. This awareness has to come from an outside source, which is middle class intellectuals.

No doubt, there are a great many Leftist journalists, who may consider that to be a none too subtle hint. Right you are! Now it is up to my "Leftist Brethren", as well as my "Leftist Sisters", my Comrades, to raise *their own* level of awareness, to the level of true Marxists. Then in turn, they can bring this awareness to the working class.

In conclusion, fellow Leftist journalists, we will know we are accomplishing our duty, when the signs and posters, the slogans spoken by all working people, is:

Dictatorship of the Proletariat!
Scientific Socialism!
Workers of the World, Unite!

CHAPTER 22

CONCERNING STOCHASTIC TERRORISM

The American public is being exposed to the term "stochastic terrorism" lately, as the mainstream press is currently accusing Trump and his campaign officials of using that tactic.

In this they are correct, but that in no way changes the fact that most readers are not familiar with the meaning of the expression. It is also a fact that countless working people are closely following the so called "presidential campaign", so that this requires a little explanation.

In technical terms, it is a reference to the attempt of people to use disgust, to incite violence. This generally involves the use of "hate speech", in which a group of people are "dehumanized and vilified". It is then far more likely that others, and in particular the less advanced members of the working class, will respond with violence, attacking those poor unfortunates.

This is nothing other than one of the methods of rule, of the monopoly capitalists, the multi billionaires, the bourgeoisie. This particular method is commonly referred to as "divide and conquer". It is considered to be a "time honored" tactic, that of dividing the enemy, to have them fight among themselves, instead of fighting their common enemy.

In this case, the "enemy" being divided, encouraged to "fight among themselves", is the working class, the proletariat. The monopoly capitalists are making every effort to have workers fighting workers. In the past, this tactic has proven to be quite successful.

It was Trump who first accused Haitian immigrants, in the city of Springfield, Ohio, of "eating the dogs and cats" of the residents. Then his "running mate", J.D. Vance, the individual he chose to run for the office of Vice President, perpetuated the lie. As Vance stated:

"The American media totally ignored this stuff, until Donald Trump and I started talking about cat memes. If I have to create stories, so that the American media actually pays attention to the suffering of the American people, then that is what I am going to do".

This calls for another explanation, as a great many people are not aware of the definition of the word "meme". According to the internet, it is "an amusing or interesting item, such as a captioned picture or video, that is spread online, especially through social media".

To think that J.D. Vance, an individual who could well become the next Vice President of the United States, considers the accusation that "Haitian immigrants are eating the cats and dogs of Springfield", to be a "meme", an "amusing or interesting item", speaks volumes concerning his character. That man is nothing short of contemptible!

It is to the credit of a certain mainstream journalist, that he pointed out the lies and hypocrisy of these racist lowlifes:

"They know it is a lie, yet they are defending their racist hate speech, concerning Haitian immigrants in Springfield, Ohio, which is ripping the community apart, and sparking violent threats…. J.D. Vance openly admits to and defends lying about Haitian immigrants eating pets…. Admits that he made up the violent smear against Haitian immigrants in Springfield Ohio, in order to create a meme, that the mainstream media had to report on".

It is significant that this particular "mainstream journalist", admits that the "mainstream media", was *forced* to "report on" this particular "meme", even though it was clearly a lie! So much for the mainstream press being fair and impartial!

This brings us to another term, which the mainstream press is using, that of "dead catting". This is a rather disgusting reference to a "shocking or dramatic and usually false claim", in order to "distract from a more damaging story", according to the internet.

Strangely enough, it has its origins in the entertainment industry. In cases where a stand up comedian was "bombing", it was customary to "throw a dead cat" onto the stage. This crude form of entertainment was apparently effective. It distracted the audience from the comedian, and frequently provoked a laugh.

It is reasonable to assume that the sight of a "dead cat", was not the reason for the laughter of the audience. It is far more likely that the people were shocked and appalled, and used laughter to cover their embarrassment and disgust.

Just as the entertainers of yesteryear did not hesitate, to resort to vulgarity and disgust, so too, Trump and Vance also embrace such tactics.

This brings us to yet another term, that of "Hybrid Warfare", or "Grey Zone". It is a reference to the tactics pursued by those who are completely devoid of principle, those who maintain that the "end justifies the means". They do not hesitate to stoop to any lie, fraud or deception, in order to achieve their desired goal.

In the case of Trump and Vance, the goal is the White House. If that goal involves instigating the murder of countless innocent immigrants, working class people, one and all, then so be it.

It is important to bear in mind that such behaviour is not limited to Trump and Vance. It is characteristic of all monopoly capitalists, imperialists. All are devoid of principle. All imperialists are completely reactionary. In the case of Trump and Vance, it just happens to be very open and clear cut.

This should be presented to the working class, as a clear cut example of that reaction. Those two are not exceptionally reactionary. They are merely exceptionally stupid.

Our goal is to raise the level of awareness, of the proletariat, to prepare them for the approaching revolution, and the subsequent Scientific Socialism, in the form of the Dictatorship of the Proletariat.

This can only be accomplished by becoming involved in that which interests them. At the moment, they are taking a keen interest in the "presidential election". That is the reason I am focused on that election.

We must respect the beliefs of the countless working people, those who still believe in the "democratic process", as put forward by the monopoly capitalists.

For that reason, we must encourage them to "take the capitalists at their word", in order to "change the system from within".

What better way to "change the system from within", than by demanding that they abide by the law of the land, the Constitution? After all, every elected politician in Washington, has taken an oath, "to preserve, protect and defend the Constitution". They do not get to pick and choose!

Of course, I am referring to the Twelfth Amendment to the Constitution, which lays out the procedure to be followed, in all *federal elections!* Procedures which have *not* been followed, *since the days of the Civil War!* For that reason, all federal elections, for the last hundred and fifty years, have been *fraudulent!*

As I have documented this in previous articles, there is no need to copy the Twelfth Amendment here. Suffice it to say that experts on Constitutional law should be encouraged to challenge the forthcoming federal election, on the grounds that it is Unconstitutional, as it does not follow the procedures outlined in the Constitution.

There can be no doubt that the working people of America, will pay close attention to such a court case. In this way, their level of awareness will be raised.

Equally without doubt, the ruling class of monopoly capitalists, the multi billionaires, the bourgeoisie, will be forced to change their method of rule. They are in charge, and fully intend to remain in charge!

In this way, they will be more exposed. The working class people will see them as the liars and hypocrites, that they are. As such, they have to be overthrown.

It is just a matter of time before the working class, even the less advanced strata of the proletariat, comes to realize that those of us who are Marxists, true Communists, are correct. The precise length of time largely depends upon us. It is up to Communists to raise the level of awareness of the proletariat.

We will know we are being successful, when social media proclaims:

Workers of the World, Unite!
Dictatorship of the Proletariat!
Scientific Socialism!

CHAPTER 23

DANGER OF REGIONAL WAR IN MIDDLE EAST

In 1948, certain members of the Jewish faith, those who refer to themselves as Zionists, managed to create a separate state for themselves, referred to as Israel. It is their belief that God gave them the "Holy Land", otherwise known as Palestine, and that all non-Jewish people should "vacate the premises".

Prior to this, within Palestine, for hundreds of years, people of various religions had lived there, largely in peace, respecting the beliefs of one another. The creation of the state of Israel, brought that mutual respect to an abrupt end.

The geographical area of the state of Israel increased in 1967, as a result of the "Six Day War", in which Israel went to war with the Arab states of Egypt, Syria and Jordan. This resulted in the capture of the Sinai Peninsula, Golan Heights, Old City of Jerusalem, West Bank and Gaza Strip.

The people of Palestine consider all of Palestine, to be "Occupied Territory", which is to say, occupied by that which they refer to as the "illegal state of Israel". Most Arab states are also of that opinion. Yet the mainstream press refers to the West Bank and Gaza Strip as the "Occupied Territories", so that the title is wide spread. For that reason, for the purposes of this article, I have chosen to use those titles.

The state of peace and mutual respect, which existed in Palestine before 1948, changed dramatically, at the time of the creation of the Zionist state of Israel. All of those who were not of the Jewish faith were removed from their homes. The polite term for this is "ethnic cleansing". Most of the "Displaced People", or "Palestinians", were forced into tiny, overcrowded enclaves, or "Occupied Territories", currently referred to as the "Gaza Strip" and the "West Bank". These "Territories" are ruled by the government of Israel.

Many of these "Displaced People" were formerly farmers, proud people, growing their own crops. Now they are confined to the Occupied Territories, largely degraded, without land, reduced to the level of beggars, relying heavily on "hand outs". Of course they are resisting!

Various political groups have taken shape, both within and without the "Occupied Territories" of Palestine. All are united in their determination to destroy the state of Israel, which they maintain is an "illegal state". In this way, they are determined to achieve the liberation of the people of Palestine.

Perhaps the most well-known is the Palestinian Liberation Organization, the PLO. Then there is Hamas, mainly active in the Gaza Strip. Hezbollah is mainly based in southern Lebanon. The Houthis are mainly based in the state of Yemen. Together they form the "Axis of Resistance", although the Israeli's tend to refer to them as the "Axis of Evil".

The experience of the Six Days War, has taught all of these various groups, a valuable lesson. The Israeli military, referred to as the Israeli Defence Force, the IDF, is very powerful. Not to be under estimated. It is supplied **with** the latest American made arms and equipment. The troops are also well trained. Yet they can be beaten.

It was the Vietnamese who defeated the Americans, through the use of "guerrilla warfare". This is a reference to "irregulars", or "civilians", those who are not part of an official army, but specialize in ambushes, traps, raids, sabotage, as well as "hit and run" tactics. The use of tunnels is an integral part of guerrilla warfare.

For a great many years, those who are "Anti Zionists", opposed to the state of Israel, have been preparing to go to war with that state. This includes the arming and equipping of various "irregulars", as well as the digging and utilization of countless "underground bunkers", or tunnels.

As well, the state of Iran is well aware of the fact that the Israeli air force is armed with the latest American aircraft. The Iranian aircraft are old and out dated, no match for the modern F35's. So they are not about to challenge them, or at least, not in aerial combat.

Instead, the Iranians have focused on developing missiles. Quite successfully too, as the events of October 1, have proven. On that day, almost two hundred missiles were launched from Iran, onto the military targets in Israel, hundreds of kilometres away. Many of those missiles hit their targets! Long range, powerful and accurate! Most impressive!

Some of these missiles were "intercepted", or "shot down", by the Israeli defence, the so called "Iron Dome". This is a reference to a very elaborate, "high tech", radar controlled, computer activated, missile defence system, in which missiles are used to intercept missiles. On that day, the Iron Dome was largely ineffective.

The Iranians were able to "pierce" the Israeli air defences, with the use of "hyper sonic" missiles, those which are able to travel at over five times the speed of sound, or greater than "Mach 5".

Bear in mind that "Mach" is a reference to the speed of sound, so that Mach 5 is five times the speed of sound. Technical jargon!

The precise amount of damage, of this missile strike, is not clear, but it is widely considered to be considerable. It is very likely that a great many American made, F35 jets, were destroyed.

Now the Israeli's are faced with war on "numerous fronts", to use the jargon of the military. On the one hand, they are faced with the guerrilla warfare of Hamas and Hezbollah, and on the other hand, the conventional warfare of Iran, in the form of missiles.

As I write this, the mainstream press is focused on the "response" the Israeli's will take, to this missile strike. All journalists are agreed that the only question is the "form of the retaliation", as Israel "goes up the escalation ladder". Journalist jargon!

Most of them are of the opinion that Israel will not strike the nuclear sites of Iran, partly because they are so well defended. Besides, they are largely deep underground, or buried in mountains.

As well, President Biden has expressed his disapproval. Not that the Israeli's pay much attention to that which Biden says. A mere "barking dog"!

Most of those journalists are agreed that Israel will likely strike the Iranian oil sites, including refineries, storage facilities and oil fields. These are referred to as "soft targets", less well defended, easily struck, with a minimum of risk, and maximum damage.

In particular, Kharg Island has been mentioned, as a likely target of "Israeli aggression". It is a huge oil terminal, described as being "critical for the oil exports of Iran".

If indeed Israel does choose to retaliate, in this manner, then it is reasonable to assume that Iran will respond, in a similar fashion. In fact, numerous oil facilities, throughout the Middle East, including within those countries which are allied to America, may soon find themselves engulfed in flames! One good turn deserves another!

Those same journalists are concerned that this will "have a catastrophic effect on the world economy". Typical! A war, in which countless people are being killed and wounded, in danger of expanding and becoming a "Regional War", and all they can think about, is the "world economy"! They are merely concerned with the profits of the capitalists!

This "Local War", which could soon escalate into a "Regional War', has further implications. After all, reliable reports are that Iran and Russia may soon enter into a "Mutual Defence Act".

Bear in mind that Iran is suspected to be within six months, of developing no less that ten nuclear weapons. And they certainly have the missiles to deliver those nuclear payloads! Not to mention the fact that Russia has no shortage of "nukes"!

Perhaps a certain former American president was correct, when he expressed concern about a possible "Third World War"!

Even if those warring countries resort to "nukes", that does *not* mean "Armageddon"! It does *not* mean that "Judgement Day" is upon us! It *does* mean that we have our work cut out for us!

While we have to respect the beliefs of all common people, including those who believe that such is indeed the case, we have to encourage such people to persevere. Now is not the time to sit back and wait for the world to come to an end! Now is the time for action!

Nuclear weapons are indeed terrible. As are machine guns! Rockets! Artillery! In fact, all gun powder is capable of inflicting terrible damage! Which it does!

It is the monopoly capitalists, the multi billionaires, the bourgeoisie, which are behind these wars! They are only too happy- even anxious! - to have working people fighting each other! The more butchery the better! Divide the proletariat, and increase profits! A win- win situation! Their "cup runneth over"! Who cares if the weapons used are "nukes"?

This particular class of people, the monopoly capitalists, the bourgeoisie of various countries, must be stopped. They are completely reactionary! They will not hesitate to slaughter millions of people, in an attempt to increase profits! The experience of two world wars leaves no room for any doubt, on that point!

It is up to the working class, the proletariat, to overthrow the monopoly capitalists, the bourgeoisie. It is the class which is *destined* to perform this noble task! Now it is a matter of making them *aware* of this fact. That is where conscious people, those who are aware of the existence of classes, and the conflict between the classes, comes into play. In other words, Marxists, true Communists, those who call for the Dictatorship of the Proletariat, *must* bring this awareness to the proletariat.

As I have mentioned in previous articles, the proletariat is not aware of itself, as a class, complete with its own class interests. For that reason, in the struggle with the class of monopoly capitalists, I can only compare this to that of two boxers, one of whom is blind folded.

Of course, the boxer who is blind folded is the working class, swinging wildly in all directions, as it is not class conscious. The boxer who can see very well, the monopoly capitalist class, is supremely class conscious.

It is the *duty* of Communists, to "remove the blind fold" from the working class, to *raise* their level of awareness, to make them *class conscious*. They, or at least the most advanced members of the proletariat, must be raised to the level of true Marxists, embracing the Dictatorship of the Proletariat.

Now, more than ever before, the situation is most urgent. The current war in the Middle East, is expanding, threatening to become a "Regional War", if not a "World War".

To the people involved in these wars, the classification makes little difference. They just want these wars to end.

That which I am suggesting, is indeed a "tall order", but completely manageable. Bear in mind that the middle class is "living on borrowed time", as the multi billionaires have recently decided to wipe out that class. The fact is that all businesses but five, are "Too Small to Succeed". Even General Motors is "Too Small to Succeed"!

If nothing else, even if only in the interests of "self-preservation", may I suggest that middle class people read once again, the Essential Works of Lenin. This time *without* the bourgeois bias, as is taught in University. You may find yourself surprised to find that everything Marx and Lenin said is true!

Perhaps even more surprising, you may find that you have a bright future under Scientific Socialism, in the form of the Dictatorship of the Proletariat. As opposed to capitalism, under which you have no future whatsoever!

Rest assured, your skills in organization and in running a business, will come in most handy, after the revolution. You will be in demand, and paid accordingly.

But first is the "not so little detail", of overthrowing the class of people who are determined to destroy you. Of course I am referring to the bourgeoisie. It may help to think of this as, "Ain't payback a bitch!". As they are so determined to wipe out your class, feel free to take part in the destruction of their class, the bourgeoisie!

With that noble goal in mind, regardless of the motivation, feel free to focus on raising the level of awareness of the working class, the proletariat. As most working people are now cultured, complete with digital devices, that makes the task so much easier.

Feel free to flood social media- I believe that is the correct term- with calls for Scientific Socialism, for the Dictatorship of the Proletariat. Share your previous experience as a capitalist, and the lessons learned from this. Take part in creating Councils, also known as Soviets, in serving the working people. Your past will not be held against you!

Encourage working people to join the two mainstream political parties, as card carrying members. They can also run for office, as members of those parties! Take the capitalists at their word! Try to change the system from within!

Lest we forget, remind all working people that the Twelfth Amendment to the Constitution, lays out the procedure to be followed in all *federal elections!* Encourage experts in Constitutional law to challenge the 2024 "presidential election" as *Unconstitutional!*

Celebrities must become politically active! Especially Hollywood "movie stars"! Strangely enough, your adoring fans pay strict attention to you! Share your experience! That includes any possible sexual exploitation and degradation! Be creative! Entertain! That is your department! Education through entertainment!

The preceding was merely a few suggestions, concerning the manner in which we can prepare the working class, the Proletariat, for their approaching Dictatorship. The need is urgent, and the tools consist largely of the internet. With the proper application of those tools, the situation can be quickly turned around.

We will know that we are being successful, when certain expressions are wide spread, among the working people, as well as on the internet:

Dictatorship of the Proletariat!
Scientific Socialism!
Workers of the World, Unite!

CHAPTER 24

ISRAEL AND AMERICAN IMPERIALISM UNDER ATTACK

The mainstream press is reporting deep concern, over the possibility of the current "conflict" in the Middle East, expanding into a "Regional War". Their fears are well grounded!

The "conflict", to which they are referring, is nothing other than a series of wars, which are raging in the Middle East, against the state of Israel.

For over a year, within the tiny Gaza Strip, an area occupied by Israel, the Israeli Defence Force, IDF, has been trying to wipe out the political party known as Hamas. Unsuccessfully, I might add, as the resistance continues, with over forty thousand residents killed, most of whom are civilians. These people are referred to as Palestinians.

To the north of Israel, in Lebanon, the group known as Hezbollah, has been firing rockets, missiles and drones into Israel. The IDF has responded by sending in jet aircraft, bombing suspected Hezbollah sites. As well, they recently sent troops into Lebanon.

Yet another group, known as Houtis, based in Yemen, has been active mainly in the Red Sea, firing missiles at cargo ships, disrupting the shipping in that vital Sea. There have also been reports of missiles being fired at American warships. The Americans have responded by bombing suspected Houti camps, in Yemen.

These groups, or "Islamic Resistance Parties", are considered to be "proxies" of Iran. They are thought to be armed and equipped by Iran, and supposedly operate on behalf of the Iranian government.

Then on October 1, the Iranian military confirmed the worst fears, of western analysts. The country launched nearly two hundred ballistic missiles, at Israel. Many of these missiles "pierced" the Iron Dome defence system, causing considerable damage to military installations, airfields, radar sites and intelligence centres.

Without doubt, Iran has spent many years developing a most impressive arsenal of "projectiles", drones and missiles of various sorts. Some of these drones may even have adapted "stealth technology", in that they may be "invisible" to enemy radar. Many of them have managed to fly into Israeli airspace, undetected.

The American military has responded to this, by sending in their own missile defence system. This is referred to as "Terminal High Altitude Area Defence", THAAD, complete with American personnel, to man the system.

This is referred to as having "boots on the ground". American boots, on Israeli ground, subject to attack by "enemy combatants", which is a reference to Iran, or any one of their "proxies". Truly, this could well lead to Regional War!

The question that naturally comes to mind, is just why America is so determined to defend Israel. In order to properly answer that question, we must first face the fact that capitalism, which came into existence with the birth of the industrial revolution, was at first competitive, and possessed certain progressive characteristics. As I have covered this in earlier articles, there is no need to repeat it here.

That changed, and changed quite dramatically, at the time that capitalism reached the stage of monopoly, around the beginning of the twentieth century. The bourgeois economists of the day, knew that something had changed, that it was no longer the old time competitive capitalism, which they had learned to know and love. This "new capitalism" was referred to as "imperialism", otherwise known as "monopoly capitalism".

The task fell to Lenin, to examine this new stage of capitalism, and explain its features. This he did in 1916, and wrote a masterpiece, titled Imperialism, the Highest State of Capitalism.

There is one passage, which I have chosen to quote, as it is of particular significance. It explains the behaviour of the warring imperialist parties. In reference to the colonial policy of the capitalist countries:

"As there are no unoccupied territories - that is, territories that do not belong to any state…. we must say that the characteristic feature of this period is the final partition of the globe - not in the sense that a *new partition* is impossible - on the contrary, new partitions are possible and inevitable - but in the sense that the colonial policy of the capitalist countries has *completed* the seizure of the unoccupied territories on our planet. For the first time the world is completely shared out, so that in the future *only re-division* is possible; territories can only pass from one 'owner' to another, instead of passing as unowned territory to an 'owner'". (italics by Lenin)

The United States, America, claims the Middle East as "their own". The country of Israel is nothing other than their "proxy". They use Israel to "exert their influence", throughout the Region.

Now the people of Palestine are in revolt, demanding national independence. Their friends and allies, in neighboring countries, are offering their assistance. All are determined to wipe out the illegal state of Israel, as well as driving out the American imperialists.

The country of Iran has distinguished itself, as one of the few countries in the Middle East, to stand up to American imperialism. It has further distinguished itself, in the tactics it is using. The missile attack it launched, against Israel, focused on military and intelligence targets, rather than civilians. This is to their credit. Way to go, Iran!

There is a strong possibility that this war will escalate, to a "Regional War", involving all of the Middle East. As there are United Nations troops in Lebanon, American troops could find themselves fighting UN troops! As well, several North Atlantic Treaty Organization countries, NATO, have openly sided with Iran. This could lead to Americans fighting the very organization they founded!

Now the various countries within the Middle East, many of which are feudal monarchies, are "considering their options". They very likely see the "writing on the wall", that Iran is about to drive out the Americans, and that it is "prudent" to "jump ship", to "throw in their lot", with the Iranians. Hence the diplomatic maneuvering.

Now it is up to American citizens, common people, both middle class and working class, to "do their part", and not just as a show of support for the people of Palestine. After all, those "local wars" could soon become a "Regional War", with American troops and ships attacked. It is also entirely possible that nuclear weapons could be used.

At the risk of being accused of being a "panic monger", bear in mind that the Korean Peninsula could also break out into open warfare, at any time. The tensions are reported to be "extremely high", with the military forces on "high alert". There are thousands of American troops in South Korea.

That brings us to the "self-proclaimed" island "country", of Taiwan. China maintains that Taiwan is nothing other than a part of China, and fully intends to "bring it back into the fold". The Americans are equally determined to keep it separate from China. The American fleet is stationed close by, in case of a "Chinese invasion". This could happen at any time.

It is entirely possible that Americans could soon find themselves fighting a war, *on three fronts!* All in the interests of securing the profits of the multi billionaires, the bourgeoisie. American working people are expected go to war with people they do not even know, with whom they have no quarrel, just so that the country can control those colonies!

This is to stress the sense of urgency in the current situation. As I have documented in previous articles, there are various ways that people can become active.

Among other things, these include becoming involved in Councils, or Soviets, assisting, arming and training working people, in preparation for the insurrection. The "presidential election" should be challenged, on Constitutional grounds. Join the two mainstream political parties, as card carrying members, and run for office. Celebrities can publish videos, calling for Scientific Socialism. Take part in the creation of a true American Communist Party, Dictatorship of the Proletariat.

As I have gone into this, in more detail, in other writings, there is no need to repeat it here. Suffice it to say that the imperialists have to be defeated, before they drag the country into a devastating war, one that could bring America to ruin.

Now that the capitalists have blessed us with the internet, and the subsequent "social media", it is only proper that we should express our gratitude, by using this new technology, against them. We no longer have to rely on pamphlets, posters and banners, to get our message to the public. We can use emails and videos, which tend to be far more entertaining. May I suggest flooding social media with calls for:

Dictatorship of the Proletariat!
Workers of the World, Unite!
Scientific Socialism!
Prepare for Insurrection!

CHAPTER 25

CONCERNING THE ELECTORAL COLLEGE

There are 538 Members of the Electoral College. Each and every Member of that Electoral College is appointed by the fifty states, as well as the District of Columbia. As the name implies, it is the **duty** of these Electors to elect the President, as well as the Vice President, of the United States. A majority of 270 **votes** is required to secure either office.

It is these few Electors, and only these Electors, who have been entrusted with the election of the next President, and of the next Vice President. That responsibility is not to be taken lightly.

Yet certain journalists, including those who consider themselves to be Leftist, are openly scoffing at the Electoral College. They are referring to it as "idiotic", and "farcical". Such is hardly the case. On the contrary, it is the *law. Constitutional Law!*

I am of course referring to the Twelfth Amendment to the Constitution, which was enacted into law, in 1804. It was the slave owners who were responsible for the creation of **the** Electoral College, as a means of voting in one of their own, as President. His name was Thomas Jefferson.

For that reason, we can say that the Electoral College is a *remnant of slavery!* Yet it remains in effect! We can further say that there are a great many people in Washington, including *all elected federal politicians, all Members of the House of Representatives, all Members of the Senate,* who have taken an *oath,* to *"Preserve, protect and defend the Constitution"!*

Those same people do *not have the right* to "pick and choose". It is their *duty* to enforce the Constitution! All of it! It is not a mere "scrap of paper"! That includes the Twelfth Amendment!

Yet as I have documented in previous articles, that is precisely what they are doing! They are carefully disregarding the Twelfth Amendment!

In the interest of avoiding any misunderstandings, I must add that their reasons for this may be none but the finest. After all, it is a remnant of slavery, and should be abolished. But until such time as that happens, it is the "law of the land", and must be respected.

Now we are faced with the rather "peculiar" situation, to put it politely, in which each of the fifty states, appoints Members of the Electoral College, as is required by Constitutional Law, and in particular, the Twelfth Amendment. So far so good!

The "peculiar" then takes place, starting with the appointment of Electors, from the District of Columbia. The Twelfth Amendment makes no reference to any District! It states, "The Electors shall meet in their respective states"! The appointment of Electors, from the District of Columbia, is in violation of Constitutional Law!

Even more "peculiar" is the fact that all states, as well as the District of Columbia, have laws that require each Elector, to vote for the candidates, for the President and Vice President, of one of the two mainstream political parties.

The states have *no right to meddle in a federal election!* The Twelfth Amendment is clear! "The Electors shall vote by ballot for President and Vice President …. they shall name in their ballots the person voted for as President, and in distinct ballots the person voted for as Vice President".

It is up to the Electors, to vote for the "person", of *their choice,* for the office of President, as well as the "person", of *their choice,* for the office of Vice President!

It is up to the states to appoint the Electors. It is in turn, up to the Electors, to elect the President, and the Vice President.

There can be no doubt that all Electors are highly respected, well-educated residents of the various states, as well as the District of Columbia. Equally without doubt, all of those same Electors are being disrespected! They are being treated as "common messengers", similar to "carrier pigeons", sent to Washington to "rubber stamp" the candidates for office, of one of the two mainstream political parties. In *direct violation of Constitutional Law!*

The Electors have every right to be upset, as they are being treated with the utmost contempt. They are highly trained professionals, responsible for the election of the highest ranking federal officials in the country, the offices of President and Vice President.

Yet may I suggest to the Electors, that now is not the time to "get mad". Now is the time to "get even"!

The law is on your side! The various state laws, which require you to vote for the candidates of one of the two mainstream political parties, are *Unconstitutional!*

With that in mind, I have a word of advice. *Stand up! Grow a backbone! Defend the Constitution! Perform your duty!*

May I further suggest that all Electors get in touch with one another, through the internet, of course. The idea is to agree upon an individual for the office of President, and also agree upon an individual for the office of Vice President.

I realize that is a "tall order", and will likely not happen. Not all Electors are likely to be in agreement. Yet all that is required, is a simple majority of 270 Electoral Votes. If no one candidate receives that majority, then the matter goes to the House of Representatives.

As the Twelfth Amendment states, "If no person have such majority, then from the persons having the highest numbers not exceeding three on the list of those voted for as President, the House of Representatives shall choose immediately, by ballot, the President".

This is my somewhat less than subtle way of encouraging the Electors to put aside their differences, at least temporarily, in the interests of democracy. If you people cannot decide, then it will be decided for you. To put it somewhat crudely, "Use it or lose it"!

As I have previously pointed out, the "November Presidential Election", is a farce. As it is not mentioned in the Twelfth

Amendment, it has no legal bearing. It matters not in the slightest, whether Harris or Trump, wins that "Election".

This is not to say that the monopoly capitalists, the multi billionaires, will not fight the Electors, should they choose to perform their duty, and vote for the individuals of their choice. We should be so lucky!

We can only hope that many Electors will do just that, and not vote for the candidates of one of the two mainstream political parties.

Strictly as an example, a majority of Electors could vote for a certain Senator, from the state of Vermont, one who classifies himself as an "Independent Socialist", for the office of President. Those same Electors could also vote for a certain Member of the House of Representatives, a member of "The Squad", regarded as a leader of that little group, for the office of Vice President. Or the Electors could vote in reverse order. Either way, the next President, as well as the next Vice President, would be "Leftists".

It is doubtful that the monopoly capitalists, the multi billionaires, would tolerate such a thing. They could even charge those Electors, for violating state laws. The courts, or at least the Supreme Court, would in turn strike down those state laws, as Unconstitutional. This is precisely what we want!

The results of the 2024 federal election, are of secondary importance. The main thing is to raise the level of awareness of the working class, in preparation for the forth coming revolution, and the subsequent Scientific Socialism, in the form of the Dictatorship of the Proletariat.

All working people, as well as a considerable number of middle class people, will have to become convinced, from their own experience, that the multi billionaires, the class of people known as the bourgeoisie, are in charge, and fully intend to remain in charge! As almost all Americans are closely watching the federal election, we can use this to our advantage.

As I write this, the "November Election", otherwise known as the "Popular Vote", is still a few days away. It has the attention of countless people. We can use this to our advantage, as a means of exposing the lies and hypocrisy of the monopoly capitalists.

I can only hope that concerned citizens, those who are at least interested in democracy, get in touch with each other, through social media, and support all of the Electors. Let them know that we "have their backs". Perhaps experts in Constitutional Law can offer to represent them, if the need arises.

At the same time, be sure to include in your messages, the following slogans:

Workers of the World, Unite!
Scientific Socialism!
Dictatorship of the Proletariat!

CHAPTER 26

SUPPORT THE ELECTORS!

November 5, 2024. Presidential Election Day in America. A day which will "live in infamy", if you will excuse the expression. The day a former president, a multi billionaire, a convicted felon, has once again won the Presidential Election. Donald Trump is now the "President Elect", soon to be sworn in as President, on **January** 20, 2025. *Unless he is stopped!*

This little task is perhaps, not as difficult as it first appears. After all, the "Presidential Election" is *completely fraudulent! Unconstitutional!*

Now the 538 Members of the Electoral College are about to be *degraded!* Each of these Electors is a proud professional, a respected member of the middle class. Yet each is about to be treated as a "common servant", forced to "run an errand", to cast their ballots for one of the sets of candidates, of one of the two mainstream political parties, for the offices of President and Vice President. In *complete violation of Constitutional Law!*

Of course I am referring to the Twelfth Amendment to the Constitution. That is the Amendment which lays out the procedure to be followed, for all *federal elections*. There is *no Presidential Election!* The American voters have *nothing to say* concerning the election of the President, or the Vice President! That is strictly at the discretion of the Electors, the Members of the Electoral College!

It may be objected that the Twelfth Amendment, and the subsequent Electoral College, is a "remnant of slavery", and should be abolished. True! Yet at the moment, it remains part of the Constitution, and must be respected. The Constitution is not a "scrap of paper"! There is a *process* to be followed, in order to change the Constitution.

This is referred to as "democracy", and without doubt, the American democratic republic is under attack.

It is the multi billionaires, the monopoly capitalists, the class of people known as the bourgeoisie, who are responsible for this assault on democracy. Trump just happens to be one of their own. That in no way changes the fact that he is a mere "figure head", a "puppet". The monopoly capitalist *class* "call the shots", and Trump "dances to their tune".

The polite term for this is "class struggle", which is to say the struggle between the bourgeoisie and the other classes, most notably the working class, the proletariat, but also the middle class, the petty bourgeois. A more accurate term is "class warfare", as the class struggle is about to break out into open class warfare! The bourgeoisie has just announced that it plans to *wipe out the middle class!*

For the benefit of those who are skeptical, bear in mind that *all businesses but five*, and *all banks but seven*, are *Too Small To*

Succeed! As these banks and businesses fail, the "small business owners" -including the owners of General Motors! - are about to go the way of the dodo bird!

A considerable number of middle class people are already painfully well aware of this, and are making preparations for the approaching "disaster". They are buying gold and silver, and hiding these "assets", in safe deposit boxes. As if that is about to do a "world of good"! Mere "stop gap" measures!

Allow me to offer a friendly little word of advice, to those worried middle class people. Your fears are well grounded. Your days of a comfortable existence, as members of the middle class, even upper middle class, are "numbered". Consider yourselves to be "living on borrowed time". Very soon, the stock market will crash, the banks will fail, all small businesses will "follow suit", and the country will enter a Second Great Depression.

At that point, your standard of living will "nose dive". You will have to abandon your multimillion dollar houses and apartments, or "condominiums", if you prefer. Their value will drop to negligible. As well, the "used car lots" will be cluttered with luxury vehicles, of little value. Other status symbols, such as those "hundred thousand dollars" watches, will be sold for "next to nothing", at the pawn shops. The Auction Houses will be flooded with works of art, so that they will be sold at a fraction of their original value.

You will find yourself poverty stricken, forced into the ranks of the working class, the proletariat.

Under those circumstances, any gold or silver you may have "tucked away", will not last for long. It will soon run out. Feel free to consider the alternative.

That alternative lies in embracing the revolutionary theories of Marx and Lenin. Face the fact that the working class is *destined* to overthrow the completely reactionary class of monopoly capitalists, the bourgeoisie, and *crush* that class, under the Dictatorship of the Proletariat.

Now is the time to *join* the proletariat, in the war against the bourgeoisie. As they have just declared war on your class, this only makes sense. We have a common enemy. Our main goal now, our "key link in the class struggle", is to complete preparations for the approaching Revolution, which includes the Insurrection, and the subsequent Scientific Socialism, in the form of the Dictatorship of the Proletariat.

As I have gone into this, in considerable detail, in other articles, there is no need to repeat it here. Suffice it to say that, with your considerable business skills, you have a bright future under Scientific Socialism, while you have absolutely no future under capitalism.

Part of that preparation, involves immediately supporting your middle class Comrades, the Electors. Let them know that they are not alone. Advise them to take a stand! A principle is involved! Your democracy is under attack! It is their *duty* to vote for the individuals, of *their choice,* for the office of President, as well as the office of Vice President. No one has any right to force them to vote otherwise! All state laws, to that effect, must be challenged, and struck down, by the Supreme Court, as Unconstitutional! Those attorneys who are experts on Constitutional Law, can testify to that fact!

Time is not on our side. As yet, we still live under a democratic republic. That could all change in January, as the first thing Trump plans to do, as soon as he is sworn into office, as President, is set himself up as Dictator. Then Project 2025 will "swing into action"! At that point, all Americans can "Kiss their Democratic Republic Goodbye"!

That will make the task, of the democratic forces, far more difficult.

Bear in mind that it is not my intention to scare anyone. I am merely stating the facts. It is the bourgeoisie that has decided to wipe out the middle class. Take them "at their word". They are not joking. After all, they do not have a sense of humor.

Having said that, the "other side of the coin", so to speak, is the fact that American women, have recently proven themselves to be excellent organizers. They have done it before, on short notice, and now must do it again. It is very likely that they have learned from their mistakes!

Now the *immediate goal* is to convince the Electors to vote for the individual for President, of *their choice!* There is a very reasonable chance that the women can persuade *all of the Electors,* to do just that! After all, those ladies are not to be under estimated!

If even 270 Electors vote for an individual, other than Trump, then that individual *must be sworn in as President! Constitutional Law!*

Yet another possibility is to have no one candidate win a majority of 270 Electoral Votes. In that case, as *less than 270 Electors* voted for Trump, and no other candidate received the required majority, then the *Federal Election must,* by *Constitutional Law,* go to the House of Representatives.

Even that could be regarded as a "partial victory". If nothing else, it would prove, to the working class, that the multi billionaires, can be beaten! They are *not all powerful!*

Regardless of the manner in which the Electors vote, the *fundamentals* will not change. The *class of people,* known as the bourgeoisie, will remain in power. Further, they will remain determined to wipe out the middle class, "one way or another".

It is reasonable to assume that the leaders of the women's protest movement, are all middle class. Bear in mind that the bourgeoisie are determined to wipe out your class. Further bear in mind the fact that Trump is merely the figure head. Stopping Trump from becoming President, is merely the first step. It is the *class* of monopoly capitalists, that has to be overthrown.

The Women's Protest Movement, against Trump, eight years ago, was most impressive. Yet now we are right back where we started! *Half measures!*

Apparently, the leaders of that previous Women's Movement were persuaded to form a corporation. If true, it means that they "sold out". It also means that new, more resolute, class conscious women must assume leadership roles.

I am well aware that it is not right, or fair, to place this burden on American women. All such women "have a full plate", and this is the last thing they need. Yet American men have as yet to "rise to the occasion", to assume a leadership role, so that this new American Women's Movement, may serve to motivate them.

Perhaps these modern day American women can take some comfort and inspiration, from their Russian counterparts, of February, 1917. At that time, under the rule of Tsar Nicholas -Nicholas the Bloody! - the ladies of the capital city of Saint Petersburg, cold and hungry, decided they had had enough. Their "menfolk" were either dead, or in the army, fighting the war, for the sake of their "Lord and Master", the Tsar.

Those heroic Russian women took to the streets, demanding bread, as their families were starving. The factory workers noticed this, and numerous factories shut down, as the workers joined the protesting women.

The local police were ordered to "quell the uprising", but were unable to do so. The government then sent out the Petrograd Garrison, to restore "law and order", but many of the troops wavered, reluctant to open fire on their "countrymen", many of whom were women. This same Garrison then proceeded to join the "protesters".

This was the beginning of the Russian Revolution of February, 1917. As the army joined the "protesters", it rapidly became a full blown Revolution. Tsar Nicholas was forced to "abdicate the throne", within a few days.

It is significant that this Russian February Revolution, was *started* by women! It was then *carried through,* first by factory workers, proletarians, and then by the army, as soldiers "switched sides".

The similarities, between Russia of 1917, and America of today, are striking. Countless American men are in the army, at least *preparing* to fight the wars, for their "Lords and Masters", the multi billionaires, in the interests of increasing profits. Other men are busy working two and even three jobs, trying to "make ends meet". Hunger is common place. As is addictions and overdoses. Gang violence is the rule, not the exception, with the local police reduced to the level of impotence. Mass shootings are commonplace. Homelessness is wide spread. Those who are able to live in vehicles are considered to be more "fortunate". A *Revolutionary situation!*

Now is not the time for despair! Now is the time to seek inspiration from the heroic Russian women of 1917! They "blazed the trail", set the example, which we can all follow. They challenged the authority of the "all powerful" Tsar! These few, unarmed women, set out to destroy the Russian Empire, and they succeeded! But only because the workers joined them, followed by the military.

Now is the time for action. Aside from the immediate goal, of stopping Trump, from being sworn in as President, other duties demand our immediate attention.

Efforts to arm, train and equip members of the working class, led by Councils, in preparation for the approaching Insurrection, must be intensified. That Insurrection may well be forced upon us, sooner than we had anticipated. Trump may well make sure of that! The better prepared we are, the more likely we are to succeed.

The creation of a true Communist Party, Dictatorship of the Proletariat, must also be accelerated. People need leaders! Every effort must be made to raise the level of awareness of the proletariat, to make them aware of themselves as a class, complete with their own class interests, in opposition to that of the monopoly capitalists. That is the role of the Communist Party!

There is a reason that I stress the importance of the proletariat. Because it is the one and only *consistently revolutionary class!* The other classes tend to vacillate, at best. At worst, they are counter revolutionary, referred to as "Contras".

Bear in mind that both Marx and Lenin were middle class intellectuals. They turned their backs on a comfortable middle class life style, and chose instead, to work in the service of the common people, both workers and family farmers.

The point is that *certain individual members,* of the middle class, can and will become dedicated Marxists, Revolutionaries, Communists. Certain others will not. They will remain loyal to the monopoly capitalist class, referred to as Contras. Still others will vacillate, siding with the Revolutionaries one day, but siding with the Contras the next, hoping for a return to the "good old days". Even though those days are gone, *never to return!*

Now it is up to certain members of the middle class, those who are *class conscious intellectuals*, to bring the awareness of classes, and the conflict between the classes, to the working class, the proletariat. This is necessary, as the conditions of life, of the working class, do not lead to the awareness of themselves, as a class.

This awareness has to come from an outside source, and that source is middle class intellectuals.

As I have mentioned numerous times before, it is only in University that the Revolutionary theories of Marx and Lenin are taught, and then only with a view to distorting those theories. Further, as it is mainly only members of the middle class, who can attend University, it is mainly only middle class people, who are aware of those theories.

Our support, of the Electors, will certainly assist in raising the level of awareness of the proletariat. The "Presidential Election", and especially the "Election of Trump", has caught the attention of the vast majority of people. In the process of exposing the lies and deception, by the bourgeoisie, involved in this fraudulent election, the working people will become more class conscious.

By all means, feel free to flood social media, with class content, as well as Marxist slogans, in order to "spread the word":

Workers of the World, Unite!
Dictatorship of the Proletariat!
Scientific Socialism!

www.ingramcontent.com/pod-product-compliance
Lightning Source LLC
Chambersburg PA
CBHW032055020426
42335CB00011B/357